I0629126

STORIES FROM THE RABBIS.

STORIES FROM THE RABBIS

BY

ABRAM S. ISAACS, PH. D.

WILDSIDE PRESS

INTRODUCTION.

THE rabbis, whose sayings are recorded in the Talmud and Midrash — writings that stretch over about a thousand years — were admirable story-tellers. They were fond of the parable, the anecdote, the apt illustration, and their legends that have been transmitted to us, all aglow with the light and life of the Orient, possess perennial charm. The common impression that they were rabbinical Dryasdusts—mere dreamers, always buried in wearisome disputations, abstruse pedants dwelling in a solitary world of their own—is wholly unjust. They were more than ecclesiastics — they were men; and their cheerful humanity forms the secret to their character. Their background was rather sombre—temple and nationality destroyed, a succession of foreign taskmasters, a series of wars and persecutions that would have annihilated any other race. But if the Roman drove his ploughshare over the site of Judæa's capital, the Hebrew spirit refused to submit to the yoke of any conqueror. In the storm and stress of centuries the rabbis preserved a certain buoyancy and even temper, which sprang from the fullness and sunniness of their faith. They thought and studied and debated; they worked and dreamt and cherished hope—

> " Like a poet hidden
> In the light of thought,
> Singing songs unbidden
> Till the world is wrought
> To sympathy with hopes and fears it heeded not."

The rich harvest of rabbinical stories that survive can be traced to rabbinical buoyancy. It is a quality not peculiar to the rabbis; it is distinctly Oriental. Nor can absolute originality be claimed for their graceful and suggestive legends; they are children of various climes, these floating fairy tales, and the history of their migration from land to land, and literature to literature, is as enchanting, perhaps, as the stories themselves. But in Palestine and Babylonia they received a coloring that was essentially rabbinical, and were applied by the rabbis to the circumstances of their day. In their hands they became instruments of instruction that formed the solace and inspiration of the Jews in every clime. The rabbis were preachers *par excellence.* In the school and synagogue they found the story the best sermon. They taught in parables.

The Talmud is by no means merely a digest of conflicting legal opinions; it is rather a literature extending over nearly a thousand years, and embracing views on every branch of thought by as varied a body of men as ever assembled in such a long parliament of almost ten centuries. It has its mountain peaks, cold, sterile, fog-enwreathed, inaccessible save to the chosen few; but it abounds none the less in lovely meadows, bright with the sunshine of humanity and redolent with familiar flowers, with the blue sky ever near. There are grave disputations by the doctors of the law, profound dialectic harangues, bristling with the logic of the schools, which an ordinary person would not have the presumption to understand ; but, happily, there are cheerful anecdotes and sayings that never lose their interest and appeal to a common humanity. The history of the Talmudic era is written in a minor key for the Jew, but the Talmud itself is far from being a lamentation. The rabbis of old Judæa blessed God in seed-time and harvest, in sunshine and rain, in joy and sorrow, and in the flash of the lightning, in the fragrance of the rose. Such was their moral earnestness, so pure and gentle and beautiful their optimism in centuries of continuous chastening, that of them can it be truly said, they found "tongues in trees, books in the running brooks, sermons in stones, and good in every thing."

In the present volume a modest sheaf of arrows is gathered from the rabbinical quiver. Their aim is simply to entertain—primarily the select but constantly widening circle of those interested in Oriental themes, and then the intelligent reading public that will perhaps find something novel at least in these stories, which illustrate some phases of life and thought in old Judæa, and yet are not wholly foreign to the culture and tendencies of our own age. Nor are they without a certain educational value for the young, embodying virtues which must always be emphasized. Their atmosphere is one of genial humanity.

The stories, which strive to be true to the spirit of the olden masters, deal with characteristic traits of rabbinic thought and fancy. Old favorites are seen to assume a new guise; here are Faust, Margaret, and Mephisto hand in hand; here is Rip Van Winkle, a philosophic recluse, and a Baron Munchausen spins his strange fancies unchecked. The great Solomon on his magic throne weaves his enchantments and becomes a victim to their spell; and Elijah the prophet proves the mysterious friend of mankind in his everlasting wanderings. The three-leaved clover, mystic and all-powerful, of love, learning and benevolence, is made the subject of various tales. Some light is thrown upon the daily avocations of the rabbis, and their regard for labor and its blessings ages before the dawn of our industrial era. As a kind of after repast are given a few crumbs from rabbinical table-talk that illustrate the varied wit and sententious wisdom of the sages.

———

Some of the stories appeared originally in the *Atlantic Monthly, Sunday School Times, Harper's Bazar*, and other periodicals, but have been revised and largely rewritten in their present form.

———

PREFACE
TO SECOND EDITION

THE interest these stories have aroused has led to a second edition, enlarged and improved, which, it is hoped, will meet with a no less favorable reception.

A. S. I.

New York, Sept. 1911.

CONTENTS

STORIES FROM THE RABBIS

THE FAUST OF THE TALMUD.

SOLOMON the King was in despair. The divine word had been pronounced that no iron was to be employed in building the Temple, and how was he to erect a suitable edifice without the aid of iron? How could he crush huge masses of marble? how split adamantine rock? how cleave hard boulders of wood? The work had to be done. It was his duty and privilege as David's son. The resources of a mighty realm were at his service; but without the employment of iron he could not advance a step. Was he, the sovereign of Israel, to abandon the undertaking? Were his wisdom and his wealth in vain?

"Let my counselors be summoned," the monarch said. And he laid his perplexities before them. All were silent when Solomon concluded his recital. They, too, shared his chagrin and realized their helplessness. "Can none of you aid me?" the King exclaimed.

"O King!" said at length one of the sages, "there is something mightier far than iron. In the early days of creation, when light and darkness struggled for the mastery, the Almighty called into life a tiny worm, *Shamir*, which possesses the property of splitting the hardest rock."

"And where lurks this worm?" Solomon impatiently asked.

"Ah, your Majesty," the sage exclaimed, "there is the difficulty. No mortal spirit has yet discovered its hiding-place."

"That shall not baffle me," Solomon rejoined. "I am more than mortal."

He dismissed the assembly. The courtiers and sages departed, but no sooner had their footsteps died away than Solomon, arising from his throne and gazing at his dazzling signet-ring, upon which was written the ineffable Name, summoned to his presence two genii. With a rushing as of a mighty wind and a rumbling as of an earthquake they bowed before him.

"What is thy will, O master?" they ex-claimed.

"Tell me where can I find the Shamir."

The genii trembled. "Ask us not, O mas-ter. It is our king alone, Ashmodai, who knows its secret abode."

"And where does Ashmodai live?" Solomon inquired.

"Far, far from here," they replied. "Our monarch dwells upon the crest of a lofty moun-tain. He has dug out a deep pit, which he has filled with water, and covered with a huge stone securely sealed to the ground. Daily he ascends to heaven and returns to earth. Then he closely examines the seal to see whether any one has touched it and uncovered the well. Afterward he opens it himself, quenches his thirst, covers it again, and reaffixes the seal."

"Enough!" cried Solomon. "Ye can go." And with a rushing as of a fierce hurricane and a rumbling as of a mighty earthquake, the genii de-parted. In a moment Solomon called his trusty captain, Benaiah, the hero of a hundred battles. He told him what he wanted, gave him certain directions, a chain, and a seal upon which was

stamped the ineffable Name, and in addition
some wool, and various skins filled with wine.
He then bade him farewell, with many a secret
prayer for his success.

The warrior's journey was long and toilsome.
When Solomon traveled he rode upon the wind.
Seated on his mantle of green silk, sixty miles
in breadth and sixty in length, the king would
journey with the rapidity of lightning. He
could breakfast in Damascus and enjoy his
evening meal in Media, so swift was his flight
from east to west. Not so Benaiah. Many
days passed before he reached the designat-
ed path. And how desolate the mountain!
how profound the stillness! how steep the
ascent!

Nothing daunted, Benaiah set to work. He
dug out a second pit a little to the right of
Ashmodai's, drained off the water, and plugged
the opening with wool. Then he dug out
another pit, higher up, whose channel led to
the emptied pit of Ashmodai, and therein he
poured the wine.

His work completed, Benaiah looked around
with satisfaction, and hid himself behind a

stump of wood, while he awaited, full of impatience, Ashmodai's arrival.

The sun sank, the shadows of evening began to fall, and the stars shone out in their niches in the firmament. Ashmodai flew down from heaven, examined the seal, and finding it untouched, raised the stone and descended into the well. What fragrance assailed his senses! It was wine, joy-dispensing wine! Shall he taste it, or spurn the temptation?

"Wine is a mocker," he exclaimed, and was about to fly from the spot. "But wine rejoiceth the heart," was his next thought, and he could not flee. A great burning thirst overpowered him. He quaffed whole mouthfuls of the intoxicating drink. Again and again he strove to break from the spell, but the fumes of the liquor were too enticing. His brain became confused; he staggered and fell. Deep sleep claimed him for its own.

Like a flash Benaiah sprang from his concealment, and fastened the chain around Ashmodai's neck.

Ashmodai awakes at length. He perceives the chain, and in his terror and anguish

utters so wild a lamentation that the mountain trembles. In vain he strives to free himself. His eyes emit sparks of fire; his lips
are white with foam; his convulsive struggles
are frightful in their agony. The birds fly
from the scene; the stars fade in the distant
sky.

"Be patient, O mighty spirit," Benaiah exclaimed. "Thy struggles are useless. The
ineffable Name is upon thee. Be still!"

Ashmodai heaved a sigh so profound that
all creation heard and trembled; and the genii
of the sea and the air flew into their innermost
caverns, where they bewailed the fate of their
master.

"I am calm," said Ashmodai at last. "I shall
obey thy will."

Benaiah bade him follow, but wherever he
went, destruction seemed to be his companion.
Uprooted trees and overturned houses marked
his path, as if he wished to wreak vengeance
on nature. He passed a wedding party, and
he wept at their joy. "In three days," said he,
"the bridegroom will die." They hear a man bid
a shoemaker make his shoes last for seven

years, and Ashmodai bursts into laughter. "In seven days," he said, "that man may die, and he orders shoes for seven years!"

King Solomon's palace was gained at length, and Ashmodai was brought face to face with the monarch.

"I ask but this of thee," Solomon exclaimed: "I am to build the holy Temple, and need the Shamir. Tell me where it is concealed."

"I have it not," Ashmodai answered. "It is intrusted to the Prince of the Sea, and by him confided to a fowl, who is bound by a most solemn oath to retain it unharmed for all time. High on a solitary mountain-top the fowl has made his nest. He never forsakes the spot. Seek for him, O King."

Again Benaiah was summoned and again he set out on a toilsome journey. Over hill and sea he wandered, across forest wastes and pathless meadows; and at last, upon the summit of a mountain so near the sky that the star-gleams seemed reflected on its rocky sides, he discovered the fowl's nest. With a cry of joy he started forward, and placed a glass over the nest so that the fowl could see but not touch its brood. He then concealed himself behind a rock.

He had not long to wait. Soon the fowl came to the spot, and finding the hard glass, was about to apply the Shamir to split it, and thus gain access to his brood, when Benaiah uttered a startling cry. In alarm the fowl dropped the Shamir, which was caught in triumph by Benaiah, and given in due course to Solomon.

The Temple was completed, and Ashmodai still was held in bondage. Solomon rioted in his glory and strength. What treasures did he gather, what palaces erect, what magnificent cities establish! The world was ransacked to add to his pleasures, yet he was never satisfied. His ambition, his pride, his love of grandeur and extravagance, were unquenchable.

"O King," said Ashmodai, one day, as he noticed Solomon in a restless mood, "thou art become, thanks to my help, the mightiest of mortals. But, chained as I am, my powers are limited. Set me free; intrust to me but for a moment thy signet-ring, and I shall make thee still mightier."

The King heard, and full of boastful pride, handed him the precious ring, and struck off the chain that bound him.

The air grew black without the palace hall. A huge hissing made Solomon turn pale. Ashmodai rose to an immense height. His feet touched the earth, but his head reached the sky. He hurls the ring into the sea; he casts Solomon a thousand miles away. Then, with the utmost unconcern, he dons Solomon's robes and assumes the monarch's privilege.

Thus began the tragedy of Solomon's wanderings. As a beggar, unknown and uncared for, he traveled from land to land.

"Good people, kind people "—this was his constant cry—"do not pass me by. I am Solomon, King of Israel."

" Thou art king of beggars," was the answer, and he turned from the jeers and imprecations that followed him like a plague.

Tortured by the memories of past grandeur and stung by the spectacle of present neglect, he resolved to visit his capital once more.

Hope sweetened every privation and converted each hill that he climbed into the smoothest sward of green. The stars that shone above seemed to utter songs of unspeakable joy. The trees whispered fresh courage. The nearer he approached Jerusalem the more exultant his mood, until, as he entered its busy streets, he flung himself to the ground and kissed the sod at his feet.

"I am Solomon, King of Israel," he exclaimed to the people hurrying by.

A chorus of jeers was the rejoinder. Spurned by the populace, thrust from his palace gate, despised and rejected, Solomon turned in despair from Jerusalem; and one evening, as its towers were bathed in the moonlight, he began his wanderings anew.

Toward the royal city of Ammon he betook himself, and soon arrived at the palace, at whose gate he knocked as humbly as the lowest slave in the realm.

"Take pity on me," said he, in tones of entreaty, as the gate was opened. "I am starving and foot-sore from travel. I am willing to do any service for a little shelter."

"I do need help," the royal cook exclaimed. "Enter, and thou canst abide with us."

It was Solomon's duty to carry wood, to draw water, and perform other menial service, but the cook quickly noticed that the man was superior to such work. He loved to talk of higher things, and would gather the royal retainers in the twilight and discourse to them of nature in its beauty and power, of plants and their changes, of animals and their haunts. He spoke of trees, from the cedar of Lebanon to the hyssop that springeth from the wall, and he told the hidden lore of the stars, and all with such grace that the servants began to esteem him, and the cook made him his assistant. The dishes that Solomon prepared pleased the King, and he was appointed chief steward. How the household rejoiced at his advancement! but none with greater pride than Naama, the lovely daughter of the King, a fair and stately maiden, whose heart had gone out to Solomon. And Solomon reciprocated her affection; he sang to her thrilling songs of love. He compared her beauty to Jerusalem, and bade her turn away her eyes

lest they might undo him in their splendor.
He prayed for the shadows to flee and the
day to dawn—the shadows of servitude and
the day of restoration to his throne. Then,
as his tones of sadness made her countenance troubled, he changed his mood and
exclaimed,

> ' Set me as a seal upon thine heart,
> As a seal upon thine arm,
> For love is as strong as death."

The secret of their love could not long remain
concealed. Despite Naama's entreaties, Solomon was condemned to death, and it was only
her mother's tears that influenced the King to
sentence him instead to lifelong exile in the
desert.

In the solitude of this wilderness Solomon's heart was chastened at last, his proud,
boastful spirit purified. God seemed nearer to
him in his loneliness than when he reveled in
Jerusalem. Was it his pure love for Naama
which had worked the change, or his long-con-
tinued wanderings and sufferings? He felt a
different man. Hope sprang anew in his heart,

not of power or earthly aggrandizement, but a
hope of higher things—wisdom, love, righteousness.

" I thank thee, my Creator," he cried, as he
bowed in prayer. " Thou hast taught me the
lesson. Thou art the King of kings alone.
Blessed be Thy holy Name."

Full of peace, although his raiment was tattered, he left the desert and entered a city by
the sea. A fisherman approached and offered
a fish for sale. He purchased it with his last
coin, and opening it, found therein his holy
signet - ring, which Ashmodai had cast into
the sea.

But little remains to be told. How Solomon
regained his regal splendor, how he married
the faithful Naama, how he confronted Ashmodai the usurper and made him vanish at
sight of the ring, how he assembled the San-
hedrim and told them all his trials and tri-
umphs—is this not written between the lines
in the *Talmud?* But while the people soon
forgot the romance and the tragedy, and the
story of the King's return became only a nine-

days' wonder, Solomon himself never lost the impressions of those years of wandering. A certain fear never left his mind; and in the night-time, so the Song of Songs relates, his couch was guarded by sixty armed men.

THE WOOING OF THE PRINCESS.

WHO could be happier than Solomon? His land was at peace, his treasury full, his power acknowledged by the nations; his fleet covered the seas; his court attracted the best and wisest of his age. Learning and science, art and the industries flourished. Jerusalem, his capital, shone with unexampled splendor; its Temple and stately edifices, public and private, were the glory of the time, and thousands of strangers drew near from all corners of the earth. It was indeed a stirring life which the streets of Jerusalem daily witnessed —the meeting place of Orient and Occident.

Yet Solomon was ill at ease despite his grandeur. His wisdom, the source of his strength, was also the secret of his weakness. Strange irony of fate! He knew all languages, spoke three thousand proverbs, many of which were to be transmitted from age to age, and sang a multitude of songs. He knew the speech of birds and beasts, the mystery of trees and flowers; all nature was at his feet; he solved its riddles and became its sage interpreter. If his knowledge had not passed these limits, all would have been well, and the clouds of unrest would have been dissipated. But it transcended things of earth, and with bold confidence penetrated the secrets of the spheres above. It was his familiarity with the stars that gave him the sharpest pang. What, then, did the stars tell him? What dreadful catastrophe was threatening his house? These golden-eyed forget-me-nots, shining in the firmament of blue so peacefully and trustfully, could they presage woe?

Solomon was blessed not only with power and wisdom, but also with a daughter of surpassing loveliness. When the evening shadows fell upon Zion's hills, he loved to sing to her his choicest song. In the morning hours, his converse with her was his sole recreation. His soul was knitted to hers with passionate tenderness. When affairs of state weighed upon him and a thousand perplexities were to

be faced, he turned to her and found relief.
She was his solace and inspiration, as was her
mother in the days of his youth, when to wed
the maiden of his heart he left throne and people, and wandered, a foot-sore pilgrim, until
he met Naama and plighted his royal troth.
How rapidly had the years passed since then!
what changes had they brought! But Solomon lived again his old-time romance as he
saw Naama's eyes in his daughter's countenance. And the princess repaid the father's
love by a daughter's devotion—he was in truth
her ideal king, for she knew the tender side of
his nature, the heart-throbbings which he must
restrain from public view.

One evening as Solomon was observing the
stars, the thought occurred to him to discover
who was destined to be the princess's husband.
Without delay he set to work: he would learn
her good fortune. Long and intently he gazed
at the constellations. Silent and profound
were his meditations in the watches of the
night; and then, just as the first dim light
spanned the far east, and the morning stars
were singing their cradle-song for the new day,

the monarch's heart felt an unaccustomed pain. He read the secret of his daughter's fate. There it stood, blazoned, all too plainly, on the fiery constellation—she was to wed the poorest man in Israel! She, a princess, and his daughter!

Solomon left his watch-tower with agonized soul. The knowledge he had gained fairly overwhelmed him. For once the rising day, which was wont to arouse his poetic powers, had for him no charm. Bird-note, flower-fragrance, the music of rippling waters, the magnificence of his surroundings, his books, songs, and favorite pastimes, palled upon him. His lovely daughter in vain strove to soothe his disturbed spirit, which first amazed, then alarmed her. Each fresh endearment only increased his irritation. Her voice, once so gentle, seemed to him as harsh as a condor's scream. Her maiden heart was troubled indeed as she noticed the change in the King, which she could not fathom nor control, and she withdrew, weeping, from his presence.

"It shall not be!" Solomon exclaimed in his wrath and consternation. "My daughter wed a beggar! A pauper's child to sit upon the throne of David ! Nay, I shall defeat the Almighty. I shall——"

There fell a sudden silence on his imperious spirit. A picture from the past arose before his vision, faint at first and then clearer and more vivid in outline. It was a king hurled from his throne on account of his insatiate pride and ambition, and doomed to wander unknown and to suffer severe privations until he had learned the lesson of self-control and confidence in the Almighty. He saw the precious ring which he gave Ashmodai, and heard the fierce yell of triumph as the demon ascended the throne, while he—Solomon the Great—sank down, down, into an unfathomable abyss. Then another picture arose in memory—the weary fugitive, spurned and despised on all sides, famine-stricken and sick at heart, until the lesson of peace was learned at last.

"Forgive me, forgive me, Almighty !" he cried passionately. "Must I learn again the fearful cost of mortal pride ? Forgive me for doubting Thy purposes and measuring my puny powers with the Infinite ! Let Thy will be done. I shall watch Thy wisdom and abide by the result. My heart has lost its anguish and its fear. I trust in Thee with my whole heart and shall not lean to my own understanding."

Upon the rocky sea-coast, far distant from the haunts of men, Solomon had a lofty tower constructed. It was surrounded on all sides by walls high and inaccessible. People wondered at the building, but Solomon, unconcerned, continued the work until it was completed. Thither one night he had the princess brought, and placed her in charge of seventy aged custodians. The princess herself could interpose no objection or resistance to the royal will. "This shall be your home," said he to the oldest and trustiest. "It is amply provisioned for years to come. There is no door to the fortress, so no one can enter without the sentinel's knowledge. Be vigilant. Keep the princess in sight every instant. Your heads shall be the price of your remissness."

The days, the weeks, the months flew by, and the princess lived uncomplainingly in her solitary abode, so firm was her trust in Solomon. She felt confident that all was for the

best, and restrained her impatience and wonderment.

One night a poor, helpless wanderer was
toiling along, tired and hungry, his garments
tattered, his heart utterly cast down. At last
he could move no further, such was his ex-
haustion, and seeking a spot to rest, he saw
the skeleton of an ox in a neighboring field.
Thankful for the shelter from the cheerless
wind, he crept inside, and with a silent prayer
fell asleep. The elements raged without, but
he cared not for the storm. He forgot his cares
and sufferings in blessed, restful sleep, and hope
struck golden chords in the witchery of dreams.

While the traveler thus slept, all unconscious
of what was preparing for him, a huge bird
with mighty pinions alighted from the distant
hills, and lifting up the skeleton with the youth
at rest, bore them aloft to the very summit of
Solomon's tower. The burden then proving
too heavy, it was set down on the roof, before
the door of the princess. Then the bird flew
away with a shrill scream, that thoroughly
awakened the young traveler. He arose in
terror, gazed about him amazed, and began to

walk up and down the roof, from which he could descry only the rocks below and the clouds above. In the distance he saw the fast-disappearing pinions of the bird that had brought him there, and a sharp pang smote his heart as the full measure of his wretchedness was realized. He was a hopeless prisoner—to what further misery was he to become a prey?

Suddenly he sees a woman advancing toward him. She is young and beautiful, and with a commanding air, yet gracious and kind. It was the princess taking her daily stroll on the roof. Astonished at sight of the youth, she exclaimed, "Who art thou? How camest thou here?"

"I am a Jew of Acco," was the reply. "It was a bird that brought me."

"But thou art tired and tattered," she continued, pityingly. "Thy face bears the marks of misfortune. Thou art troubled and suffering. Come, tell me thy history."

He told her of his wanderings, and how he had sunk to rest in the skeleton of an ox, and then of his flight through the air. How entranced did she listen to his story, admiring his courage, and sympathizing with his sorrows. She had him clothed in new garments. Her servants bathed and anointed him. Then his eyes shone with new radiance, and his whole being assumed a lovelier aspect. As they spoke and strolled together kindred tastes were revealed. For the first time the princess realized the beauty in her father's words, written decades before: "My friend is mine, and I am his;" while the youth, as he contemplated the solitary tower and the imprisoned maiden, exclaimed with Solomon: "A locked-up garden is my sister - bride; a locked - up spring, a sealed fountain."

The north wind blew, and the south wind blew. They loved, for both were beautiful to each other, and the world was before them. What should they do? Fly, and seek happiness in some distant spot far away from the king, whose anger they had now every reason to fear?

"Nay, nay, beloved!" she ardently exclaimed. "My father's wisdom would discover our hiding-place, and his chieftain, Benaiah, would drag us back to Jerusalem, to meet perhaps a criminal's fate."

"There is one resource, dearest," he rejoined after a pause. "Marry me here."

"Marry thee? Yes, that I will, but how can we marry according to the law of Israel? Where is the ink with which to write the marriage certificate? Hast thou thought of that?"

"Despair not!" was his reassuring reply. "I am prepared for every emergency." He bared his arm, and, opening a small vein, used his blood as ink, and the marriage was secretly solemnized, with the words, "May God be my witness to-day, and the angels Michael and Gabriel!"

Their spell of happiness was brief. The custodians of the princess were thrown into the wildest consternation when they discovered what had taken place. They stormed, they raged, they threatened. But it was too late to argue with the pair. No more time was to be lost, so they hastily sent the swiftest-footed of their number to the royal palace, and the story was told.

Solomon no sooner heard the announcement of his daughter's marriage than he ordered his mantle to be brought for instant use. It was of green silk, interwoven with fine gold, and

embroidered with images of all kinds. He sat
upon it, and swiftly was borne on the wind to
the solitary tower.

"Where is the youth," he vehemently cried,
as he gained entrance, "who has dared to
marry my daughter ?"

"Nay, father," the princess pleaded, "be not
angry with him. He has endured enough of
wretchedness—why begrudge him his spell of
happiness ? Reproach me, but spare him, for
love is our master, and thou didst write in thy
'Song of Songs,' 'love is as strong as death.'"

He deigned no reply to his daughter. His
thoughts were of the man who had won her
affections. "So thou art the one who has presumed to marry a princess !" he exclaimed,
scornfully, as the youth was brought to him,
showing not a trace of fear.

"Oh, King," he rejoined, calmly, "be not
too severe ! I but obeyed the words of Solomon: 'Many waters are not able to quench
love, nor can the waters flood it away.'"

"Who is thy father, and where thy dwelling-
place ?" inquired the king, softening a little at
the youth's tone and words.

"I am the son of a poor Jew of Acco," was the answer. "Altamar is his name." And his heart grieved as he thought of his family's poverty.

" What ? " almost shouted the king, while he trembled in his agitation. " The son of Altamar of Acco, the poorest man in Israel ! "

" Yes, oh, King, I am that poor man's son," and the youth for the moment lost his courage, but regained confidence as he saw the princess step forward and take her place proudly at his side, looking lovingly at him.

" He is my husband," she exclaimed in a clear, firm voice, " according to the laws of Israel. With his blood he has sealed our troth. Our union is irrevocable. A higher Power has led us on. Thou canst not part us now."

" Nay, nay, my daughter," Solomon responded, deeply moved. " He is indeed thy husband and my son," and he beckoned them both to approach nearer. " Thou art the very man who—so the stars told me—was destined for my daughter. Thy name, thy lineage, thy estate proclaim thee the same. God is the ruler of the universe : He declares, and it comes to pass. Blessed is He who giveth a wife to man."

THE RIP VAN WINKLE OF THE TALMUD.

AGES ago—it was about fifteen hundred years—there lived a man whose name was Rabbi Honi. In his busy and stirring times he loved solitude, the quiet fields, the silent hills, the lonely mountain rivulet, anything that would make him forget his daily surroundings. He liked to take long walks by himself, in such profound meditation that he heeded not the passing scene. He refused, self-absorbed, to mingle in the varied life of the world. The cheerful forge, the merry reaper, the crowded street, boys and girls at play, music and games—he would spurn all these, and far away from the haunts and habitations of men would he wander, as if this bright and blessed world had neither charm nor interest for him.

"What is life? what is life?" he asked him-

self, as with slow and measured step he crossed
the meadows, far beyond the outskirts of his
native town.   " It is like the fleeting shadow,"
so he thought; " not like the shadow of a tree,
nor yet the shadow of a wall, but like the shadow of a bird, which mounts aloft, and swiftly
flies away."

He sighed as he went along, as though he
were bearing some hidden burden, some unknown care, that changed into wretchedness
the currents of his being.   But his sadness was
converted into wonderment, as he saw an old
man planting a carob-tree.   Love and happiness beamed from that aged face, while with
trembling hands and tottering limbs he busied
himself with the task.

" Unfortunate man !" cried Honi, in a voice
of scorn, " what folly is thine !   Dost thou
waste thy feeble powers in planting a tree
whose fruit will grow in seventy years ?   Dost
thou hope to live so long ?   Poor fool, poor
fool !   It is a world of fools."

" Master," the old man replied in gentle
tones, " thou art mistaken; I plant the tree,
not for myself.   In my youth, I gathered fruit

from trees which my grandsires planted; and now I, too, would provide in this way, at least, for the happiness of my descendants. It is an innocent pleasure, on my part, and makes me happy." And the old man, with heightened color and shining eyes, continued his work.

"Happiness, happiness!" murmured Honi to himself. "What is happiness when life is so fleeting, and failure the universal law of nature? Why should we concern ourselves with the future, when our present burdens are so many, with no prospect of cessation? Why provide that our children gather ripe, luscious fruit, to make their lives happier? Will they not suffer and die, and is not our labor vain?"

Unable to answer these questions, oppressed by doubt, and wearied by his walk, Honi sank upon the grass and fell asleep with a child's unconsciousness. The sun sank to rest, and still the rabbi slept. The stars shone in the clear Eastern skies, and still he slept. Dawn broke, and midday came, and a hundred nights passed, and still he slumbered. What profound peace was his! Soon a wall of stones sprang up around him, and formed a friendly shelter that hid him from passers-by. So the years ran on with rapid tread, summer and winter, seed-time and harvest, with all their varied changes, and the rabbi did not wake, although each day the sunbeams hastened to greet his resting-place, diffused a kindly heat, and seemed reluctant to leave. Was this circle of stones his cemetery? Was the rabbi forgotten by the world, whose claims he had not recognized?

Seventy years had elapsed, when suddenly the stone wall disappeared as mysteriously as it had first originated, and the rabbi awoke. He rose to his feet a little awkwardly at the start, as if unused to much exertion. Then he rubbed his eyes, glanced in every direction, and exclaimed: "I have had a pretty long sleep. It was scarcely night when I sank to rest, and now it is almost midday. How stiff my limbs are! I must hurry home."
Somewhat dazed by the sudden glare of the sun, and with a peculiar confusion in mind and gait he set upon his way. His steps were slow and hesitating, when, seeing a carob-tree, he stood rooted to the spot. Like birds returning

to their nest, his thoughts flew back to the
scene—the old man, the planting of the tree,
his own words of scorn seventy years before.
Surprised, amazed, he approached nearer, and
saw how stately the tree had grown, with its
rich vegetation. A lad was eating of its fruit.

"Boy, boy!" exclaimed Honi, in a voice of
anxiety which was not to be restrained; "tell
me, who planted this carob-tree?"

"Not I," the lad replied, with a light laugh.
"Don't you know how long it takes such a tree
to bear fruit? Why, my father told me that it
was planted by my grandsire." And the boy
continued eating to his satisfaction, without
noticing the stranger's anxious glance and peculiar garb.

The lad's words were not lost upon Honi;
he grasped at once their true significance. He
knew at last that he had slept seventy years.
A nameless dread fell upon him as he resumed
his way homeward. But the once familiar path
had disappeared—the hills of his youth had
been leveled. The green sward, which had
yielded to his footsteps of old, had given place
to rows of houses, and the long line of spread-

ing trees, beneath which he had so often mused, was no more to be seen. The blue sky, so radiant in sunshine, seemed more distant than ever. Earth and heaven alike had changed.

He was soon in the heart of his native town, but he recognized it not. The streets, the houses, the people, were alike strange. There was not a friendly hand stretched forth to grasp his own; not a smile greeted him; not a voice gave him welcome. The multitude passed him idly by. There were curious looks directed on him, and he caught now and then a contemptuous phrase. Some countenances seemed familiar to him, but they stared coldly when he began to address them, and his heart sank within him.

"If my friends and acquaintances no longer know me," so ran his thoughts, "at least my family will not spurn me; to them I will go, and seek rest in their midst."

Buoyed up by sudden hope, he inquired of a passer-by the dwelling of Honi's family, and soon with loudly throbbing heart knocked at the door. It opened, and a scene of household happiness was revealed. There were strong, healthy lads at play, their smiling mother sharing their joy, and a man of well-knit frame plying his work. As Honi entered, the room grew silent, and all eyes were cast compassionately upon the bearded stranger, with the sad, weary countenance.

Approaching the man, Honi asked in a trembling tone, " Wilt thou call for me the son of Honi ? "

" Honi's son ! " replied the man with an astonished air. " Why, he has been dead many years."

" But who art thou, then ? " And the old man's head sank lower and lower.

" I am Honi's grandson."

With a loud exclamation of joy, Honi drew nearer his grandson, and was about to embrace him rapturously, saying: " I am thy grandfather."

But the man coldly stepped back, gazed at him a moment, and said: " Thou my grandfather ! I do not know thee ! I never saw thee ! What monstrous imposition dost thou wish to practise on us ? "

Honi then told his wondrous story of the sleep under the wall of stones, of his sudden awakening, and his return. He described his sense of desolation and helplessness, when he found himself a stranger among strangers, and he entreated them to deal with him more kindly and justly, being flesh of their flesh.

Honi's eloquence had at least one effect—it convinced his hearers of his sincerity. He evidently believed that he was the long-missing Honi, and they had not the heart to undeceive him, or openly tell him of their want of faith. They resolved to humor him, and receive him as an honored guest in the house, allowing him to do whatever he pleased.

Thus Honi returned. His story was noised abroad. He became the talk of the town. They all thronged to see him, and to learn if he really was the rabbi whose mysterious disappearance had aroused such comment at the time, to be forgotten with the new generation. The stir and inquiry, however, soon grew less, then ceased entirely, and Honi was left to himself again. The home of his youth had undergone a transformation: it was his no more. At his own hearth he was a stranger. When he had many friends, he had abandoned them, and courted solitude; now, when he yearned for love and friendship, he was doomed to solitude. The whirligig of time brings its revenges.

He strove to rouse himself as the days flew by. He would mingle with the teachers, for he had been a teacher in his time. When he met them he knew them not, nor did they recognize him. It was pathetic for him to note in the school of learning how his name was spoken with great veneration, his verses quoted, his opinions discussed, his principles referred to and made the subject of keen controversy. And he sat and listened as if he were already buried —he, the living Honi—while his eyes were full of tears.

He often wondered whether, in the years when he was concealed by the circle of stones, he was less an object of concern than now, when he breathed the air of heaven and thrice each day uttered his praise to God—at morn, midday and eve. Why had life been restored to him, if his existence was to continue a bitter mockery? Why must his yearnings and

aspirations remain ever unsatisfied? He loved
mankind, and he was spurned by men. He
delighted in the merry prattling and sunny
glances of children, and when he appeared they
ran away in fear. If in his manhood he had
preferred study and solitude to fellowship with
his kind, surely his penance had been bitter
enough. Must the punishment be everlasting?

In his despair he shunned the school and
the haunts of men with all his olden persistence.
He sought the solitude again, buried in moody
contemplation, which no effort of his could
throw aside. One morning, following a lonely
path beyond the outskirts of the town, he sank
on the ground and exclaimed: "Give me society, O God, or give me death! I am alone
on earth and my punishment is greater than I
can bear. Call me to Thyself and to peace."

His imploring prayer was not in vain. His
broken spirit soon found peace. Upon the
wings of compassion God's kiss was breathed
upon him and he slept. His life's stormy currents were calmed at last.

RABBINICAL ROMANCE.

IT might be fairly presumed that the rabbis of the Talmud lived in too troublous times and wrestled with too profound problems to give a thought to romance of any kind. But just as in later centuries among their Arab kinsmen, not all the heat of conflict could check the strains of the gentler muse, which diversify Arabic literature with songs of love and beauty, so the rabbis pause for a while in their discussions of law and practice, and lighten up the pages of Talmud and Midrash by quaint and charming pictures of romance, which appear the more beautiful when one reflects on the circumstances of their age. It was not an epoch of sonnets and serenades by any means. They had neither troubadours nor poetasters. Their school was hardly the Della Cruscan. Their tournaments were of an entirely different character; their master-songs

were of another key. The Bible was their one
epic, the prose and poetry of the people, the
standard of life, the measure of their aspira-
ration.   Its lofty ideal of marriage was preserved in Jewish jurisprudence; its divine sanc-
tion gave a singular dignity and solemnity to
the institution among the Hebrews.   The idyls
of the Patriarchs, the " valiant woman" of Proverbs, the love scenes of the "Song of Songs,"
proved the forerunners of rabbinical romance
and invested it with their own beauty and at-
tractiveness.

Of the pictures of rabbinical romance which
have been preserved, few equal in charm the
following: There appeared once before the
famous Simon ben Jochai an Israelite and his
wife who desired a divorce, as their union had
not been blessed with children.   The rabbi
received them kindly, heard their story, acqui-
esced in their resolve; but suggested in cordial
tones that, lest people might suspect them of
improper motives or attribute to them some
disgrace, the parting should be of the most
friendly character.   He bade them return home,
provide a feast for their friends, and on the

morrow apply to him for a legal divorce, which
he would cheerfully grant. The couple were
pleased with the rabbi's advice and kindliness,
and hastened to prepare a bountiful feast for
their friends. As they were getting ready for
the banquet, the husband gently said to his
wife : "For many a year, in sunshine and in
storm, we have lovingly lived together. I can
bear the highest testimony to thy faithful affection ; and on my part I have tried to prove
loyal to thee. If we separate now, it is not in
sudden anger or hatred. That is far from our
thoughts. As a pledge, then, of my warm at-
tachment, thou canst take with thee whatever
thou likest best in the house, however great
its value. It shall be thine as an everlasting
possession." The wife's eyes gleamed suspiciously, but she said nothing, assenting with
a smile to her husband's agreement. The evening arrived. The feast began. It was as bountiful as their means allowed. When, one by
one, the guests had succumbed to its influence,
and her husband, too, had fallen asleep, the
good woman had him removed to her father's
home and awaited hopefully the result. He

awoke at last from his stupor and could not understand the situation until she softly said: "Dost thou not remember what thou didst bid me do—to take away what I liked best in thy house? Well, it is my husband that I prefer to everything else. Naught but death shall part us." When the two visited the rabbi again and told him that they proposed indefinitely to postpone the divorce, he blessed the pair in his fervor, and they had sons and daughters in due course. This fond wife's expedient was imitated in after centuries by the Gülph countess, whose castle was besieged by the Emperor Conrad, and who besought as a favor that the women might be allowed to pass out unmolested with whatever valuables they could carry. Next day, when the gates were opened, every wife was seen carrying her husband and children, and the unmarried women those nearest and dearest!

Rabbi Jose had the misfortune to be married to a violent shrew, and when he found life unbearable in her society, he was reluctantly obliged to divorce her, according to the letter of the law. She married again, and the years

rolled on. Her second husband, after a length-
ened period of suffering, became blind, and they
were both reduced to such poverty that she
was compelled to lead him through the streets
begging for bread. But a feeling of shame always caused her to avoid the neighborhood of
Rabbi Jose's house. The rabbi's reputation
for benevolence having reached the blind
man's ears, he asked her why she did not lead
him thither, and when she told him the reason,
he insisted upon her accompanying him to the
rabbi's. But the poor woman's sensitiveness
was not so easily overcome, and she flatly refused to go. Without any more delay, then,
he beat her so severely that her cries attracted
a crowd of people, all eager to witness the pro-
ceedings. Amid the confusion, Rabbi Jose
appeared on the scene. Learning quickly the
state of affairs, he had their wants attended to
at once, provided a house for them, and main-
tained them out of his own meagre income.
When his inquisitive disciples asked him
whether she was not the same woman who had
previously made his life so wretched, he replied, " Yes, and for that reason I am bound

to assist her; for is it not written, 'do not shut thine eyes against thine own flesh?'" The rabbi never forgot that she was once his wife, and for the sake of his early dream of bliss, which he had never realized, his heart was filled with compassion.

It was indeed a lofty ideal of womanhood to which the rabbis paid homage. The Hebrew term for betrothal, *Kiddushin*, "sanctification," proves the high import of marriage among them. If so famous a master as Judah the Prince could permit his disciples to accompany a bridal procession as it passed the Academy, it is evident that the rabbis were no gloomy ascetics, as they have often been painted. One thinks, too, of the charming tale of Rabbi Meir's wife, of which Coleridge has given an English version that is tolerably well known, and who, to break gently the intelligence of his sons' death, compared them to jewels entrusted to his care for a few days, and then demanded back by their owner. "Pray not that sinners be destroyed," said the same wife on another occasion; "pray rather that sin perish from the earth, and that sinners repent and mend their ways." The name of this gentle universalist was Beruria. "Vex not thy wife," said Rab, "for she is easily moved to tears." "The whole world grows dark to him who has lost his first wife," writes another sage. "Who has no wife has nothing good, no joy, no blessing, no peace." "Descend a step to gain a wife." "If she be smaller than thou art, bend a little and whisper in her ear." "With zeal and solicitude honor thy wife, for it is the wife that crowns the home with a blessing." "Who is best taught?" a rabbi asked. "He who has learned from his mother." The gentle ministry of women, to which Ernest Renan has paid a tribute in his recognition of the services rendered him by his mother, his sister and his wife, is attested in the story of Ishmael ben Elisha and his mother. She loved him almost to adoration, and when he attained eminence, she strove to brighten his home life, and would insist upon performing menial duties for his comfort and pleasure, even washing his tired feet when he returned from the academy. Her unselfish ministry at last reached a point where he thought it unworthy of a mother, and he refused to submit to her patient and persistent affection. The next day she appeared in the academy, and accused her son of violating the commandment of honoring one's parents. Surprised at the charge, the rabbis asked her to explain herself, and then she related how her son, whose learning she idolized, and who was her guest as well as son, prevented her evincing the proper respect to him. It was decided that Rabbi Ishmael should obey her command as the fulfillment of filial duty.

The rabbis could appreciate valor and moral dignity as well as motherly tenderness in women. They tell that when Alexander the Great, on one of his expeditions, reached a country governed by women, he was about to attack the capital. Just before the signal to advance was given, a woman of lofty stature and noble countenance stepped bravely forward and asked Alexander what brought him to her land. When the king replied that he had come to fight and conquer, she rejoined: " Hast thou come to battle with women ? Are the men all dead, that thou wishest to display thy prowess with us ? Believe me, thou wilt find it more difficult to subjugate us than thou art inclined to fancy. But shouldst thou conquer, will it not be said that thou conqueredst weak women ? Should we, however, prove victors, think, O great Alexander, of the disgrace to thee, and of thy glory forever clouded ! Leave our country, then, and attack lands more worthy of thy arms." She ceased, and Alexander was so charmed by her courage and sense that he clasped her hand as a sign of peace and friendship, and only craved permission to inscribe the following on the gates of the capital: "I, Alexander the madman, after having subdued so many countries, have at last come to this land, and learned wisdom from women."

The rabbis liked to apply similes which Holy Writ employs, and express in a parable the relation of Israel to God as that of bride and bridegroom. There lived once—they say —a man who betrothed himself to a beautiful maiden, and then, after he had gained the pledge of her affection, he left her and went away, while the maiden in her sorrow waited for his return, but without avail. Her com-

panions and rivals mocked her and exclaimed:
" Why dost thou idly wait ? He will never
return to thee." Did the maiden abandon her
faith in the absent bridegroom ? Just the reverse. She went into her room and took out
one by one the letters in which he had vowed
his fealty. She read them again and again,
and was comforted amid her tears. And her
loving confidence was amply rewarded. He
did return at last, and when he inquired why
she had kept her faith so long and what hope
sustained her, she showed him the precious
letters. Similarly, when Israel was in misery
and captivity, she was mocked by the nations
for her hopes of redemption, and taunted with
many a bitter sneer. But, undisturbed in her
faith, Israel went into her schools and syna-
gogues and took out the letters and was con-
soled in her afflictions. In due time God, her
bridegroom, would come and redeem her,
and when He would say, " What hope has
cheered thee ? how couldst thou, among all the
nations that mocked, retain thy loyalty ?" Israel would exultantly point to the Law and
answer, " Did I not have Thy promise here ?"

THE SHEPHERD'S WIFE.

IT was the old, old story, and yet as new
then beneath the glowing Palestinian skies
as to-day in cottage or palace. He, the poor
unlettered shepherd, had the effrontery to love
his master's daughter, who had many wealthy
suitors, for her wealth and beauty had proved
powerful magnets. Hired to watch the rich
Kalba's flocks, by the subtle influence of love
alone Akiba had won Rachel's affections.
Their union, bitterly opposed by her father,
who saw all his cherished hopes and plans
thus defeated, had been finally consummated.
Kalba's threats and imprecations were alike in
vain; with a woman's insight Rachel saw the
gold in her husband's nature, she had faith in
his intellectual capacity, and went with him in
love's glad confidence. To her he was more
than a rustic clown.

From her father's magnificent dwelling,

whence she had been banished, to the wretched
hut which was now to be her home, no change
could have been greater. Delicately reared,
she was to suffer the keenest anxiety. Her
every wish had hitherto been granted, her
every desire gratified. How different was her
present outlook! But she cared not if poverty
was to be henceforth her lot. Its sharpest
stings lost their pain when she pictured to herself the happy future. The world would learn
to recognize her husband's powers, and all
privation would be forgotten. What a sorcer-
er is love—what a net it weaves! Would it
prove a dream or reality?

One day they were reduced to such extreme
want that they spent their time in picking up
straw from the barns and roadway to serve
them as a bed. The prophet Elijah, who is
ever ready to aid the loving in heart and
strengthen their affection, assumed a beggar's
attire—for he is prolific in disguises—and
knocked at Akiba's door, and it was quickly
opened. "Good people, kind people," he cried,
"give a few bits of straw to a poor and un-
happy man, whose wife is in sore distress."

"Why, dearest," said Akiba to his wife, as the stranger departed having not asked in vain, "how happy we should be! What if our means are straitened, there are people poorer than ourselves, who do not possess even a little straw. Should we not be grateful that we can aid them?"

"I do not murmur," she rejoined. "I am blessed in thy love, which many waters cannot quench, nor rivers sweep away. I do not complain, for in thine eyes I have found peace. And yet I have one wish," she continued, gazing at him earnestly; "it is that thou shouldst attain the full measure of thy strength. But I shall not be impatient or importunate. God heeds the yearning of the seedlet, and He sends His dew and sunbeam, His rain and wind, and it becomes a perfect flower. So shall He make thee a perfect man —all in His own good time."

Akiba did not and could not forget his wife's soulful words. They swiftly flew from her heart, and made a nest in his. Perhaps he had never appreciated education aright, nor cared in reality to attain eminence in the daily round of humble duties which he had to discharge. But a new desire sprang up in his soul. In his lowly avocations each day his wife's words were heard—those mute reminders of duty to be done, of work to be achieved, of aspirations to be realized. Even as King David, when a shepherd lad, had listened, entranced, to the songs of the night—star, planet, and the host of creation uniting in grateful testimony to the Divine power and mercy—Akiba's heart, too, had often been stirred as he watched nature in its silence and majesty. What doubts and questionings would wrestle with him, what ambitions struggle for utterance ! How his eyes became clearer, and his mind more certain ! How his hopes revived and strengthened, his fears diminished and passed away ! The world was full of mysteries—would they ever be explained ? Scripture was to him a closed roll—would it ever be opened ?

It chanced once, as he was thus reflecting, that he approached a wayside well, near which he noticed a stone somewhat excavated. When he asked a passer-by who had excavated the stone, he was told that it was caused by drops of water continually falling upon it. "If so soft a body," he then said to himself, "can excavate a stone, surely the precious words of the Law must more readily soften my heart, and purify my understanding. The die is cast. I shall hesitate no more. I shall attempt to realize my wife's ideal. I must sit at the feet of the sages, and drink from the well of their knowledge. I must rise above my present lowly calling, and heed the voice that bids me aspire higher. I must become a perfect man, a holy teacher in Israel, and God's mercy, which causes the flower to blossom, will aid me in developing my powers to their fullest bloom."

He quickly made known his resolve to his wife, with an exultation that was new to him. She bravely restrained the tears, as she thought of his enforced absence, and the hard struggle for existence which both must wage for years to come. She sweetened the interval before his departure by painting pictures of his success, if he were true to the voice within. The period of separation would pass as swiftly and unconsciously as a dream, and with what joy would she greet him on his return, a master in

Israel! Then her father, reconciled at last, would hasten to acknowledge his merits, and their lives would be crowned with enduring happiness.

"Oh, hasten! hasten, dearest!" were her words at parting. "Fulfill thy vocation. Become a teacher of thy people. Each day shall be a messenger of peace, bringing good tidings of thee. Dost thou not recall the prophet's saying: 'Behold, my servant shall be wise. He shall be exalted, and extolled, and raised on high'?"

For mourners the years are heavily freighted, and for lovers they fly with an arrow's speed. The seasons quickly changed; the years rapidly rolled by. Five, ten, twelve times, in the swift transformations of nature, had the early roses perfumed the wayside, and the snows whitened the hills.

From time to time vague rumors had spread of the famous scholar, who had gathered a host of disciples around him, and expounded the Law with such marvelous clearness and simplicity that all the land wondered. His explanations were couched in terms that even chil-

dren could understand. He had developed a
new system of study, which led to surprising
results. His lectures were thronged, and his
school grew illustrious from Rome to Jerusalem.
He loved to preach in parables, and his sayings
were twice-told tales, which people liked to
hear and take to heart—so beloved and ad-
mired was he.

And now he was to return, after the many
years of absence. The shepherd had become
the master. The wife's fond desire had been
fulfilled. But did he think of her when he
reached his olden home? Had he forgotten
his source of inspiration, and, buried in the study
of the Law and the sciences, lost all memory of
the faithful soul who had chosen him and poverty? Perhaps she had not survived the twelve
years' unaided struggle—she, with her delicate
rearing, her youth and inexperience, to wrestle
with hunger and want and pain? Better to
have died than to have lived broken-hearted
at a great man's ingratitude.

When Rachel learned that Akiba was expected at last, who can describe her rapture?
Her wildest hopes had been more than real.

ized; for she never had imagined that her husband would attain such celebrity. She would have been amply satisfied with modest fame, and now a world-wide reputation had been won. But perhaps he has forgotten her in the changes of the years—that often happens in human history. Perhaps he has grown to despise the wretched hut and its inmate. Will he recognize his wife and accord her a rightful place at his side ?

The day had come. The place of assembly was crowded. The towns and villages in the neighborhood had flocked to welcome Akiba. Kalba, proud and austere as of old, was there. He had never been reconciled to his daughter, and was careless of her fate. Surrounded by his numerous disciples, Akiba received the greetings of the multitude. But he seemed dissatisfied. His gaze searched far and near, and his face wore an anxious look. Suddenly, at the very edge of the crowd, he saw one whose form had always hovered near, and whose love had ever urged him on. He saw a pallid woman, in tattered garments, whose wan face lit up with wondrous rapture as their eyes

met. One swift, penetrating glance told her
that he was true, and in the intoxication of the
moment the wretchedness of years of waiting
and uncertainty was forgotten forever.

"Rachel! Rachel!" he cried, breaking impulsively from his circle of disciples, and pressing through the wondering throng. "Let her
come forward!" he shouted in loud and joyous
tones. "Rachel, my wife, the shepherd's wife,
to thee all honor is due! Thou hast made me
what I am: I and my pupils, we owe everything to thee."

"My husband!" she exclaimed, as she nes-
tled in his embrace, "now I know the true
meaning of Solomon's words, 'I am my beloved's and his desire is toward me.'"

"But thou art in tears, Rachel. In tears on
such a happy day!" he added, with the least
bit of reproach in his voice.

"Be not vexed," she rejoined, smiling.
"These are not tears of sadness at the years
that have passed, but tears of joy at thought of
the happy, happy years to come."

But little remains to be told. Kalba became
reconciled to his daughter, and gave her a con-

siderable portion of his wealth; while Akiba was crowned with the threefold blessing—the love of a virtuous wife, a large share of earthly goods, and moral and intellectual endowments.

In after years, during one of their discussions, a rabbi asked of his colleagues : "Who is to be regarded as rich ? " Various opinions were uttered as to what constituted wealth, until one authority declared that whoever possesses a hundred vineyards, a hundred acres, and a hundred servants must be accounted rich. "Not so!" exclaimed Akiba, as the memory of his early romance rose before him. " He alone deserves to be called rich whose wife is sensible and virtuous." And Akiba ever treasured that sentiment until the hour of his martyrdom, when, in defence of the Law he loved so well, he met death at the hands of the Romans.

THE REPENTANT RABBI.

IT was a proud moment for the young rabbi when, his studies ended, he left the academy with all its precious associations, and full of ardent hope, set out for his native place. He had every reason to feel the glow of conscious pride; for he had completed, with rare diligence, the course assigned, and attained the highest rank among his companions. He was familiar with the Law and the testimony in their multifold ramifications, with the uninterrupted tradition of the schools from their earliest foundations, with the best learning of his time. He had flung himself into the work with a rare enthusiasm, and his rapid progress, his industry and acumen, had aroused the undisguised admiration of his associates and the warm praise of the master, not always so appreciative. That a large amount of self-love mingled with the young man's intense feeling of satisfaction was perhaps natural. He was at an age when humility hardly enters into the composition of character. It takes a varied experience to develop the finer shades of con-sciousness.

" My pupil—nay, my master," said the head of the academy as the hour of departure arrived, "for my pupils are my masters—what advice can I give thee at this moment? Thou hast abundant knowledge; thou hast high ambition; thou hast gained our sincere esteem. These are precious gifts which God has bestowed upon thee : see that they are not abused. Re-gard them as entrusted to thee for a holy pur-pose, not thine own aggrandizement. Of all men it is the gifted teacher whose responsi-bilities are the most sacred and yet but idly heeded. Let me, then, exhort thee to observe this rule in the varied relations of life : Be pliant always as the reed ; that is, be kindly to all. And never be unbending like the cedar ; that is, unforgiving to him who insults thee. Let this principle be the angel that shall guide and guard thee on the way."

The farewells were gaily spoken, and the youth (for he was but a youth, although the dignity of rabbi had been conferred on him) began his homeward journey. He could scarcely restrain his exultation, as he rode along, at the thought of his reception in his native town and what honors would be showered upon him. It seemed but yesterday when he had left his home and kindred to study to become a teacher, and now he was returning with all his expectations satisfied, his future secure. It was a lovely morn : all nature was in sympathy with his hopes and ideals. The charming landscape at his feet, the tinted sky overhead, the fragrance of spring around him, seemed smiling harbingers of happiness to come. If pictures of his parents' delight and the pleasure of his friends arose at times before him, and recollections of childhood softened his mood, the splendid vision of his own advancement was ever present. It was an intoxicating picture that fancy wove within his brain. He felt confident that his powers as teacher and preacher would give him the highest place in Israel.

"Master, master ! " cried a voice, rudely interrupting his revery. " Master ! "

He turned angrily. Who dared disturb the golden fabric of his dream, he, the young rabbi, whom all delighted to honor ? He was in no mood for importunate suppliants at that moment.

It was a poor dwarf, crouching in the road, unsightly in face as in form. When he observed that the rabbi had turned in his direction, he repeated his salutation, only too glad that he had been noticed. He was used to contempt and solitude, but what was his surprise and pain when the young rabbi exclaimed in a scornful tone : " Tell me, have all thy townspeople as hateful faces as is thine own ? I would like to know before I resume my journey."

" I know not," replied the dwarf, cut to the quick and losing his self-control; " I know not. Go to the Artist who made me, and reproach Him for His handiwork. It was not my doing."

"Pliant like the reed "—his master's parting words now recurred to him with tenfold force —kindly to all, unforgiving to none. How had he remembered the monition ? How was he applying the last lesson he had received ?

What was the vast range of his learning, compared with the dignity of a human soul that he
had treated with such contempt?   Stung with
self-reproach, and overwhelmed by a sudden
sense of his own unworthiness, he cast himself
on the ground by the dwarf's side, and begged
his pardon with many an expression of regret.

"I was hasty. Forgive my rudeness!" he
exclaimed. "I have sinned against thee, but
I beg thy pardon."

But the bitterness in the dwarf's soul could
not be so easily appeased. The constant re-
buffs he received intensified his natural sensitiveness, and the rabbi's cutting words stirred
his resentment to a flame. He spurned the
proffered hand and made no other reply to the
rabbi's entreaties than, "Go, go; reproach the
Artist for His work. Thou art perhaps a better mechanic."

They made a strange pair on the highway,
the dwarf sullen and gloomy, followed by the
rabbi half praying, half expostulating. But all
in vain. The dwarf would not be comforted,
and the rabbi had lost his golden dreams.
Imagination had painted him as a conqueror

returning in triumph to the place of his birth; reality found him a suppliant and a penitent. The very landscape had changed; the sky no longer smiled; the birds no longer sang. His confidence had become contrition.

It was known in his village that he was about to return, and the excitement was intense. The reverence for knowledge was so general among the people that the religious teacher stood in the highest esteem, and the post of rabbi became an ideal in its way. If cities competed for the honor of Homer's birthplace, no less local pride was felt in every Judæan town in being a famous rabbi's place of nativity. That compensated for the want of other claims to worldly eminence. There was ample justification for the people's joy in this instance, because the young rabbi's reputation had preceded him, and already they felt themselves entranced by his eloquence, and inspired by his learning. The red-letter day arrived. They would not wait for his appearance, but thronged the dusty road to meet him in advance. Scarcely did they discern him in the distance when they ran forward in eager groups and blocked the way along which he had to pass, while loud plaudits filled the air.

"Peace to thee, O master!" they exclaimed, as he drew near. "Peace to thee, O teacher!"

The youth received their expressions of welcome with the deepest embarrassment. In his profound humiliation and self-abasement he knew not what to say. Strange, his silence only increased the admiration of the people, who attributed his reticence to modesty, and redoubled their congratulations.

In the meantime the dwarf had mingled with the throng, and heard the praises lavished on the young man. For a while he controlled himself, but at last his feelings gained the mastery, and he fiercely exclaimed: "To whom do ye extend such honor? Is he the Messiah, forsooth?"

"What! Dost thou not know him?" came the words from many lips. "We honor the scholar, the sage—our rabbi."

"Scholar! rabbi!" repeated the dwarf with ever-increasing scorn. "May Israel never have such teachers!"

"Man, art thou crazy?" they shouted in their surprise.

"Listen, people, and judge between me and your precious rabbi;" and he told them of the insult which he had received. It was a pitiful recital, and heard in silence. It needed no confirmation. Upon the rabbi's face, usually so bright and hopeful, they read anguish and contrition. He had covered his countenance with his hands in his abasement, but suddenly he regained his self-control.

"I have erred, dear friends," he said, firmly; "I have erred most grievously. It was a cruel, a shameless act, to reproach this poor man, and I am deeply sorry for my foolish words. It was without the least shadow of excuse; I confess it openly. What more can I do? I have asked him to forgive me, but he is as unyielding as the cedar. My hasty speech has changed my joy into sorrow, and filled my soul with unutterable grief."

"Pardon him!" the people cried, crowding around the dwarf. "Pardon him! Dost thou not see his penitence? Pardon him for his wisdom's sake."

"I shall pardon him," was the reply, after a short pause, "for your sakes, and that he may never commit again so grievous a sin."

The next day was the Sabbath. The synagogue was filled with an attentive assembly from near and far, for was not the young rabbi to preach his first sermon? It was a critical moment for the preacher, but he did not fear. He had learned more from one day's experience than from a year of study and reflection; for humility had entered his heart, and the warm gulf-stream of compassion was developing his nature to a richer maturity. He felt stronger, more resolute, more hopeful in the growing sense of dependence on One whose mercies were unending, and whose gifts were boundless. The world had broadened unconsciously—the school was receding from view. In the stir of new duties and the pressure of new conditions, how unreal and fantastic appeared life at the academy, and the interpretation of texts! He was to study men, not books, and what should be the guide? While his mind was wrestling with these thoughts, he rose to preach, and a solemn silence reigned

as he announced his text: " Be always pliant
as a reed, and be never unbending like the
cedar." But in the rabbi's heart, inspired by
new emotions and purified by the consciousness of human weakness, there was no silence;
the joy-bells of gratitude were pealing an an-
tnem to God.

THE INHERITANCE.

THE heart of Hyrcanus was full of joyful emotions. His pride and exultation knew no bounds. His fields were broad, his granaries full, his increasing flocks and herds grazed contentedly on the hillside, and a hundred youths and maidens hastened to do his bidding, and added to his rapidly growing wealth. But he was happiest when he noticed his sons hard at work at the plow or with the flail, their faces all aglow with their daily toil, and he would pass along the line with many an encouraging word.

" How happy the farmer's life ! " was his frequent remark. " He is his own master; sunlight, dew, rain, heat are his eager servants. God, with lavish hand, places fruit and flower at his feet and scatters on every side the rewards of his labor. My sons shall be farmers, too—not so, my lads ? Farmers, strong, ruddy, alert, like your sire, to continue his name to all generations. Let people talk about the joys of city life and other careers and occupations; we know how to prize our own calling and appreciate its blessings."

It happened once that, as Hyrcanus visited his fields, he observed that one of his sons, Elieser, seemed moody and dejected. When he was asked the reason of his discontent, he responded by a flood of tears.

"What ails the boy?" said the father to himself. "He does not look ill. Perhaps it is his pride, for he is the proudest of the lot. Does he think that his present employment is too menial? That fault, if it be a fault, is easily remedied. I shall have him undertake a lighter task and the smiles will come back to his countenace."

In vain. The son's sadness steadily increased, and baffled the father's solicitude. The youth would often rest from his toil and turn his gaze toward the east. Sighs escaped him, and all the symptoms of discontent. He would perform each day's task, but there was no heart in the work, and when the allotted labor was done, he courted solitude as if it had a balm for his anxious thoughts. He loved to follow the bird in its flight until it was lost to view in cloudless space. He would pluck to pieces many a flower, as though to gain the secret of their fragrance. In the peace of twilight he would leave his home, mount the neighboring hill, and commune with the stars as if they could answer his questionings or soothe his sorrow.

Now Hyrcanus had continued to observe his son's disquietude, and sought to discover the secret, but without success. One evening, meeting Elieser in tears, he said : "Come, my son. Tell me thy grief. What disturbs thee? Why is thy brow so sad, and why has thy heart, once so merry, lost its cheer? Come, tell me. Be frank, and conceal nothing."

" Oh, father, father ! " the youth exclaimed. "I will be frank with thee and conceal nothing. I hate the farm and the fields ! I yearn for something higher and nobler. I cannot endure much longer this kind of life. It is worse than a stifling prison ! "

" Well, my son, " replied the father, sadly,

"thou hast been frank, and I confess thy words have disappointed me not a little. My thoughts are naturally wrapped up in my farm, and I have always longed to have my sons follow in my path and succeed as I have done. But I would not be harsh or unkind to thee. I will change thy occupation, if it be thy desire. What shall it be, then? A saddler, a weaver, a carpenter, a blacksmith?"

"A saddler, a weaver, a carpenter, and the rest!" rejoined the youth with flashing eyes. "Why speak of them? It is only one ambition that possesses me. I would be a scholar, father; I would study the holy Law. I would devote my entire life to learning."

"So that is the secret which I have vainly sought to discover?" the father answered. "Thou wouldst be an idle scholar! At thy age, too! Be satisfied with the farm, Elieser. Curb thy straying fancy and settle down to the farmer's life. Let thy sons be scholars, but choose for thyself a more sensible fate."

A few days passed. The cloud of sorrow pressed heavier and heavier on Elieser. He grew more and more sullen. He refused his accustomed food. Sleep was denied him. But ever stronger became the yearning to study the divine Law.

"If I could only learn of the Maker of this boundless universe!" he exclaimed to himself as he took his solitary walk. "The distant star mocks me. The flower at my feet taunts me with my ignorance. The birds that troop past me have more knowledge than I. Must I endure this self-reproach forever?"

"Why weepest thou?" a Voice was heard close beside him. "What is thy sorrow? Hast thou an unattained desire? Dost thou wish to study the Law?"

"Yes, yes! with my whole heart and soul! Oh, Master, Master, satisfy me! Art thou not near to all who call upon Thee in truth, and dost Thou not give to the young birds that for which they cry?"

"If thou truly lovest knowledge," spoke the Voice, in tones that thrilled the young man's soul, "and wouldst devote thy whole life to learning, submitting to the yoke which shall be transformed into a fadeless crown, fly to Jerusalem. There is the school of Rabbi

Johanan ben Sakkai. Enter its doors — the portals stand open—and be wise."

Elieser hesitated no longer. The opportunity had come. In the impulsiveness of youth, without bidding his father and brothers farewell, he fled to Jerusalem, the city of his hopes and visions, and, entering Ben Sakkai's far-famed school, stood like a statue for a moment, and then wept aloud.

"Good youth," said the rabbi, in a kindly tone, "why hast thou given way to thy emotions ? At thy age it is not usual to give way to tears."

"Oh, rabbi," Elieser answered, "I am weeping because of my ignorance, and I have such a burning desire to study that I could not but come to Jerusalem."

"But thou hast surely learnt something, hast thou not ? " the rabbi inquired.

"Nothing, nothing !" cried the youth despairingly. "Oh, teach me, master ! Without knowledge I cannot live."

Ben Sakkai strove to reassure the trembling youth. Without asking of his home and kindred, he received Elieser as his own son, and bade him grieve no more. " Thou shalt be my pupil. I recognize thy honest heart. I have full confidence in thy ability. Thou shalt gain knowledge if thou wilt but persevere, and become a light to thy people."

The rabbi's judgment was soon confirmed. The youth made astounding progress that aroused the admiration of his comrades and teachers. Ben Sakkai was amazed at the sagacity, the reasoning skill, the intellectual grasp of his pupil, whose learning grew until he was acknowledged to be the pride of the academy and its star of greatest promise. And then Elieser told Ben Sakkai his name and lineage.

What of Hyrcanus during these years? Did he grieve for his missing son? Did he seek to discover the secret of his absence? Did he regard him as hopeless and abandon all search? His father heart might have put him on the right track had not Elieser's brothers resorted to every means to poison their parent's mind. They could not sufficiently condemn their brother's deed and ingratitude.

They dwelt upon the disgrace to the family which he had occasioned, and to prevent any reconciliation, should he return, they urged their father, again and again, to disinherit him. As he despised the farm and its occupations, he should have no share in the estate.

Resolved, at last, to disinherit Elieser, the father set out for Jerusalem, to complete the act in due legal form. He soon reached the Holy City, encircled by a chaplet of hills, and moved along its crowded streets with an air of wonder. All nations seemed to be there. Greece, Rome, and the isles of the sea sent their representatives. How different from his fields and hills were the busy thoroughfares! How insignificant appeared his houses and lands, compared to the stately edifices that lined the well-paved roads, the lofty towers that shone in the sunlight, the colossal gateways, the palatial dwellings! How tame and unsatisfying was country life after all!

"Come, Hyrcanus!" exclaimed one of his friends, "Let us visit Ben Sakkai to-day. He is our most famous sage, and all throng to hear him."

It was a gala-day in Ben Sakkai's house. He had invited to dinner a large number of the most prominent people in Jerusalem, and Hyrcanus, belonging to a family of wealth and influence, was placed next to Elieser. But the father did not recognize his son; he never thought that Elieser associated in such high circles, and then the years had changed the youth completely. Study, too, had transformed the country lad, and added a refining and maturing influence of its own.

The guests feasted merrily, and had almost ended their repast, when Ben Sakkai, turning to Elieser, exclaimed, " My son, it is time for thee to reveal thy wisdom. Rise, and speak of the holy Law."

" Nay, master," Elieser replied, blushing slightly; " the cisterns can only pour out the water which they have received. What can I say that is not already known to thee ? "

" My son," Ben Sakkai rejoined, " the fountain gushes forth an ever-living stream. Rise and speak of the Law."

But Elieser was still reluctant to address the assemblage, when Ben Sakkai, fancying that his presence embarrassed his pupil, left the hall.

Then Elieser began a dissertation on the Law and holy things, and the depth and beauty of creation, of life and its wonders, of death and its mysteries, of the world in its grandeur, and the human soul. He spoke, and his eyes shone with a divine radiance, while his voice grew wondrously eloquent. The people listened, awe-inspired. Unable to restrain himself, Ben Sakkai rushed into the assemblage, and full of admiration kissed him on the forehead, exclaiming, "Oh, blessed son of Hyrcanus! Happy Israel to have such a teacher!"

The assemblage broke into loud applause— but scarcely had its echo died away when Hyrcanus exclaimed in an agitated voice, "Of whom dost thou speak? Tell me! Relieve my suspense!"

"Of whom I speak?" Ben Sakkai, replied. "Why, I speak of thy son. I speak of Elieser, who is standing at thy side."

"My son! my son!" and Hyrcanus turned to Elieser. "Thou art indeed my missing son." And again and again he clasped the young man to his breast, while the people wondered. "Happy, thrice happy am I to possess such a son! I came to Jerusalem with one resolve—I shall be frank to avow it—to disinherit thee. But now I shall disinherit thy brethren who have traduced thee. Thou shalt be sole heir of all my wealth—that shall be thy recompense, and the proof of my affection."

"Nay, father," Elieser answered, while his voice grew gentler as he spoke; "Nay, father, let each brother have his portion. I bear them no ill-will. If I desired fields, I could pray to God for them, for He is Lord of the earth. If I desired gold I could entreat God for it. Is He not the Lord of all the wealth that is? But I hunger only for the holy Law: this satisfies me."

ELIJAH IN THE LEGENDS.

THE form of Elijah the prophet rises out of the Jewish past with all the ruggedness and grandeur of Mount Carmel, with which his name and character are indissolubly associated. Few heroes of the Bible appeal so irresistibly to the Jewish popular imagination, and are stamped with such peculiar genius. The mystery which surrounds his birth, education, and family, the suddenness with which Scripture introduces him, the intense enthusiasm that marked the beginning of his missionary work, the dangers to which he was exposed, the miraculous events in which he figures, his undaunted courage and fiery zeal, would be sufficient to crown him with a certain halo of romance. But when, as a fit complement to his earthly career, one considers the circumstances connected with his disappearance from earth, it is natural that he should be regarded as one of Scripture's most picturesque personages—just the character to be seized upon in later centuries by legend and parable, and to survive for ages in national folk-lore.

One caution is to be exercised, however, in our judgment of the post-Biblical legends in which Elijah assumes so prominent a role. As is true of rabbinical legends respecting other Biblical worthies and the rabbis of the Talmud themselves, so in the case of Elijah, it is not to be asserted that the people and their teachers believed in every hyperbolic allusion to the prophet. We distort rather than interpret the Talmud, if we fail to make due allowance for the fountain-play of Oriental metaphor. In its stories and parables, its ever-winding stream of *hagadah*, we see reproduced the arabesque in art—"a magic complexity of ornament," where "the restlessly roving fancy and the speculative understanding find their pride and satisfaction," as Lübke states it. That genius for rationalism and keen critical inquiry which, despite rabbinical reverence for tradition, is at

the basis of the Talmud,* makes me reluctant
to maintain that the historical character of the
rabbinical legends about Elijah was ever an
article of faith. They are so varied, and present the prophet in such quick and sudden
transformation scenes, that one is forced to the
conclusion that here we have to deal with texts,
not flesh and blood. It is the Elijah of hom-
ilies and exegesis, weird and shadowy, embodying the mystic, philosophic ideas of the
schools—a theological finger-post, so to speak
—which meets one in the luxuriant gardens of
rabbinical fancy. So deeply did these legends
impress the susceptible popular mind, being
largely associated with themes of theosophic
and supernatural grandeur, personal and national resurrection, and the realms of the world
to come, that they acquired a certain sanctity
and permanence of their own which defied
analysis and criticism. They are undoubtedly
on a higher grade than the Solomonic legends.

---

* And is, in fact, a trait of the Jew in every century, to
whom the pithy lines in " Faust " are applicable:

" Zwei Seelen wohnen, ach! in meiner Brust,
    Die eine will sich von der andern trennen."

It is more than burlesque and pantomime. Here is no stage-fire; here no gaudy transformation scenes, with the resources of the juggler's art and witchery. We are brought face to face with solemn mysteries of life and death and immortality—the problems that ever exercise so profound an influence and fascination.

The rabbis trace a resemblance between Moses and Elijah. The one ascended Mount Sinai, the other Mount Carmel. Both were prophets. Both condemned idolatry. There was the same mystery about their passing away; both disappeared, rather than died. Still another similarity was noticed: no one knows their sepulchre. The act of Elijah in offering sacrifices on Mount Carmel against Moses' express command to offer only in Jerusalem, is explained as justifiable on the ground of its being a work of necessity. The rabbis discern in Phinehas who slew Zimri a type of Elijah; in both cases the same zeal and courage can be observed. Elijah's twofold invocation (1 Kings xviii. 37), "Hear me! Hear me!" was to show that he employed no sorcery. Rabbinical skepticism, which denied the historical character of Job and saw in the book that bears his name only "a parable," doubted, as well, the ascension of Moses and Elijah. All opinions are recorded in the Talmud : Jewish thought was never stagnant nor one-sided.

In the rabbinical legends, Elijah is a man of peace—a gentle messenger, who preaches a religion of love and humanity. With all the tenderness of a modern saint, he comforts in affliction, he warns of danger, he exhorts to repentance. But none the less emphatically does he condemn sin and show how sin may be atoned. He is quick to give counsel; he promotes peace between man and wife; he acts as referee in legal cases; he pronounces judgment; doubtful matters await his decision, and he reveals secrets. As a further prerogative, he leads into Paradise. To protect the afflicted, too, is his special duty. Nor does he shirk any disguise or labor to achieve his object, but will appear now as a simple man, and now in the attire of a Roman officer; here as a wandering Arab, and here mounted on a horse. At some of the academies he would attend as an ordinary student and modestly join in the discussions. He takes Rabbi Joshua ben Levi in hand—a famous character of his day—and shows him his future abode in Paradise. Not satisfied with such a mark of favor, after that rabbi's death he introduces him to his colleagues in the better world.

There is little doubt that Elijah's prominence is largely due to the character assigned him by tradition as forerunner of the Messiah. His reappearance on earth, foretold by Malachi, is associated with the Messianic era. The Targum Jonathan mentions this privilege of Elijah's, "the great priest who is to be sent at the end of the captivity" (Targ. Jon. to Ex. xl. 10). The Mishna asserts the same (in Eduyoth viii); and so popular became the belief, that in the Gospel narrative (Mark vii., viii., and elsewhere), we find Jesus mistaken for Elijah as the forerunner of the Messiah.

A good deal of activity is marked out for Elijah. On his reappearance upon earth, his first work will be to summon Israel, and collect the scattered tribes, with Messiah, son of Joseph, at their head, leading them to Palestine, to fight against Æmilus, the pseudo-Messiah. Then he will arouse the dead, bring Messiah, the son of David, and restore to the Temple of Jerusalem the Shekinah and the Ark, which had been committed to his (Elijah's) care by Jeremiah at its destruction. It can readily be seen to what extravagant views these legends may give rise in the literature of eschatology. Among the Jews Elijah is not canonized: there are no saints in the Jewish calendar. In the Latin and Greek churches he received such honors and became the founder of the Carmelites. In Russian popular proverbs he directs the storms, the sound of the thunder being caused by the rumble of his fiery chariot and the lightning by its blaze. Among the Kabbalists Elijah's name is repeated with special emphasis on the exit of the Sabbath; at that time he is supposed to be seated under the tree of life and unerringly records in writing the merits of those who keep the Sabbath holy. Curious is the survival of the custom, at the Passover repast, of having an extra goblet of wine for Elijah. I am tempted to explain this as a proof and

illustration of Hebrew hospitality. All Israelites, masters and servants, men, women and
children, are alike commanded to be present
at the Paschal meal: on that evening all are
freemen; the barriers of rank, class and cir-
cumstance are thrown aside. What more natural than that an extra cup of wine should
be provided for the traveler or stranger guest
who may by chance arrive on the festival eve ?
Such a custom is quite common among rabbis
to-day, who are glad to invite a poor brother
to their Sabbath meal in obedience to the Mo-
saic law, "Thou shalt love thy neighbor as
thyself."

Once the prophet met a man who mocked at
holy things. "My son," said the sage quietly,
"how wilt thou justify thyself before thy Father
in heaven, when He summons thee to swift
and impartial judgment ?" "Oh, I know how
to answer," the skeptic rejoined, unabashed.
"Why, I shall tell God that He ought to have
given me knowledge and understanding; but
as He did not, He is to blame, not I." "What
is thy business ?" Elijah then asked, deeply
moved. "I am a fisherman," was the curt re-

ply. " Thou art a fisherman," said Elijah, "and
hast understanding enough to arrange nets, to
hurl them into the water, to watch for fish at
the proper time ! Who gave thee understanding for this ?" "Understanding for all that
sort of thing !" exclaimed the man coolly,
"why, that is nothing. Every common fisherman has it." "Nothing !" Elijah answered
with emphasis. "It is indeed something.
Dost thou think much understanding is necessary to carry out the law? 'The law,' says
Moses, 'is near to thee; it is in thy mouth, and
in thy heart, and thou canst do it.' " Touched
to the quick by Elijah's reproof, and convinced, as well, that the prophet had both
logic and reason on his side, the fisherman
wept tears of repentance and abandoned his
skepticism.

Once in the busy market-place Elijah appeared to Rabbi Beroka. Curious to pry into
the secrets of life eternal, the rabbi asked the
prophet: " Who among all this crowd will enjoy future salvation ?" " That man yonder in
black sandals, like a heathen, and without
fringes on his garments." The rabbi was not

a little astounded that one who violated the
statutes of the law should have a portion in the
world to come, and, approaching the man without delay, asked him what was his business.
" I am a jailer," said he, " and take special care
to maintain morality in the prison." " But
why do you neglect the fringes ? " " That is
very easily explained," he answered. " On account of this very neglect I am regarded as a
heathen, and become thus acquainted with the
mischievous purposes of enemies of the Jews,
and inform the Jewish leaders of any threatening evil." But the rabbi's surprise for the day
had not ended. " See those two jesters there,"
said Elijah, pointing unobserved to two figures
in the crowd. " They, too, shall be saved."
Rabbi Beroka advanced quickly in their direction, and conversed with them for a few moments. He found that they were men of a cheerful, hearty spirit, who strove to comfort the
mourner and the sufferer, and to banish their
pain, while they had often restored harmony
among people, and instilled gentle peace.
" Blessed are the peacemakers," so reads the
golden sentence in the Sermon on the Mount,

"for they shall be called the sons of God."
"Love peace, and pursue peace," said Hillel;
"love mankind, and bring them near to the
Law."

WHEN SOLOMON WAS KING.

THE historical data respecting Solomon are rather scanty, compared with the rôle he occupies as a national hero. Eleven chapters in I Kings (i.–xi.), and nine in 2 Chronicles (i.–ix.) tell the story of his life; and these are possibly extracts from works no longer extant. To compensate, however, for the meagreness of historical details, legend has made him one of its favorites, and crowned him with attributes and achievements which keep his memory green, although nearly three thousand years have elapsed since he ruled over Israel.

It is not surprising that Solomon has received such posthumous honors. His name—a prince of peace; his lineage—the son of David's old age; the auspicious circumstances under which he ascended the throne; his completion of the temple; his wisdom and magnificence; the glory and triumph of his reign; the rapid

growth and extent of his sway; his foreign al-
liances and expeditions to the far East—these
naturally wove about him a magic spell, and
gained him lasting fame. The vices that dark-
ened his happiness in his declining years, the
consequences of his disobedience to God, which
are told in Scripture's blunt and unflattering
way—these are shadows on the picture, which
have only added to Solomon's hold on the popular mind, and left a distinct impress on Jewish
national folk-lore. His later sins create, in
fact, a certain sympathy for him, so singularly
favored, and yet so deplorably weak. Who
feels not compassion at Merlin's fall? Does
not Wolsey's departed greatness arouse our
pity? The appalling inconsistency between
the wise sayings in Solomon's proverbs, and
his unrestrained extravagance at last; his sub-
lime dedication prayer to the one God, and his
erection, in after days, of seats of worship for
strange gods—such contrasts and contradic-
tions show Solomon's humanity at least. It is
the humanity in "Faust" which made Goethe's
creation a world-drama. Possibly the same cir-
cumstance has contributed largely to Solomon's

popularity. We see a parallel to this in the
traditional view, among the Arabs, of Haroun
al Raschid. His reign is held to have been a
golden era, and his fame and deeds are celebrated in tuneful verse. Yet this monarch led
far from a model life, and the poets have con-
siderably exaggerated the glories of his sway.

Solomon has been aptly regarded as the rep-
resentative of Oriental wisdom. The Bible tells
us of his knowledge of nature and its produc-
tions, of his intimate acquaintance with the
animal world, his "three thousand proverbs
and one thousand and five songs" (1 Kings v.
12). Legend, first in the Midrash, and then in
still more extravagant and grotesque form in
Arabic and Persian literature, has reared an
Aladdin's palace of fancy on the simple Biblical
foundation. The ruler of Israel appears almost
unrecognizable amid the play of hyperbole.
His legendary history becomes a series of magical metamorphoses; we imagine ourselves in
a land of marvels; it is, in fact, the atmosphere
of the *Arabian Nights :*

  "Sounds and sweet airs that give delight and hurt
    not."

He flits in and out with the suddenness and agility of friend Harlequin in the olden pantomime. Jewish and Arabic sources are full of his conversations with animals; his intercourse with spirits; his power over the world of demons; his weird transformations in pursuit of wisdom—in the style of the mediæval Arab caliph—his strange adventures on sea and land. He is accompanied by a retinue of genii, who do his bidding at wondrous speed. The recurrence of types in legend as well as nature is curiously exemplified in the Talmud, making Solomon, in one of its most characteristic tales respecting that worthy, a prototype of Faust, whose Mephistopheles is Ashmodai, king of the demons; while, to render the resemblance still more striking, a Margaret is not absent from the story in the person of the lovely Naama, daughter of the king of Ammon. Naama's future, however, is happier then Gretchen's. Apocryphal literature fairly reveled over Solomon; what we possess is but a fragment of what has been written in his glorification. There seems to have been no limit to the imagination of writers in those days. Side by side with accounts of his power and grandeur, are tales of his misery and degradation. He is a beggar as well as a monarch in folk-lore. In the heat of his ambition he loses his precious ring, and wanders and suffers until he regains his ring and throne. In the height of his fame, he receives warning of impending danger; and when intoxicated with pride is made to realize the truth of the lessons embodied in the Proverbs and Ecclesiastes ascribed to him.

To select a few of the Solomonic legends, and to present them briefly, is no easy task: so many are equally striking that it is difficult to discriminate. Perhaps the most curious are those associated with the Queen of Sheba. The Bible tells of her visit to Solomon, attracted by the stories of his wisdom, and how she proposed riddles which he so readily solved. Riddles were special favorites among the ancients, and some current conundrums date from gray antiquity. If the riddle was the form chosen by the oracle in Greece, one need not wonder that the Queen of Sheba adopted a similar device to divine Solomon's wisdom.

The post-Biblical legends tell us the exact character of these riddles and their solution. When the Queen placed two wreaths before the monarch, and asked him to tell which was real, and which artificial, he opened a window, and a bee, alighting upon the natural wreath, told him what he wished to know. She brought into his presence a number of male and female servants dressed alike, and wished him to tell who were men, and who were women. He ordered his eunuchs to give them nuts and roasted corn, and the men put them unabashed in their garments, while the women, more modest, received them in their handkerchiefs, thus revealing their sex to Solomon. "What is that," asked the Queen, "which comes like dust from the earth, whose food is dust, which is poured out like water, and which illuminates the house?" "Naphtha," came the ready answer. "What cries in a heavy wind storm, and bends its head low, suffocates the criminal and clothes the wealthy, is destruction to the fish and pleasure to the bird?" "Flax," was the reply. So astonished was the Queen at his prompt and accurate answers that she exclaimed, "I did not believe what I heard of thee, until I came and saw with mine own eyes."

Once when Solomon desired to build the temple, he sent to Pharoah with a request for artisans. The king of Egypt summoned his astrologers, who told him which of his artisans would die during that year, and these he sent to Solomon. But the latter's wisdom enabled him to detect the plot, and providing each with a shroud, he returned them to Pharoah, with the message: "Hast thou no shrouds wherein to bury thy dead? Here I have provided thy men with them." When Solomon married the daughter of Pharoah, the rabbis say, she not only made him acquainted with a thousand different kinds of musical instruments, but taught him, as well, the chants to idols, which caused him to forget the worship of the One God. Solomon is represented as riding on the wind, seated upon a great mantle sixty miles square. One day he was boasting of his power and his wisdom, when the wind withdrew from him, and forty thousand men fell from his mantle. "Return," he cried in his alarm to the wind, "and be calm!" "Return to thy God," the

wind replied, " and boast not of thyself. Then
I will return." Thus Solomon was taught wisdom by the words of the wind.

In Arab legend, Solomon's sagacity was illustrated when he was a stripling of thirteen.
Two men came before David as chief of the
tribunal, and puzzled him greatly in reconcil-
ing their differences, until he asked his son
Solomon to decide. The plaintiff had bought
property of the defendant, and while digging
out a cellar had found a treasure. He demanded that the defendant should take the
treasure back, for he bought the property without it; while the defendant asserted that it did
not belong to him, as he had sold to the plaintiff the property, and all its contents. Solomon
suggested that the best way to settle the dis-
pute would be for the plaintiff's son to marry
the defendant's daughter, and take the treasure
as their own. On an other occasion, when the
point at issue was the damage done by sheep,
David decided that the owner of the field
should receive the sheep as compensation.
But Solomon gave it as his opinion that the
plaintiff should keep the sheep, receiving their

milk, lambs and wool, until the damage inflict-
ed had been made good. The other judges
were not satisfied with Solomon's decisions,
and resolved to subject him to a public exam-
ination to test his fitness to act as David's
successor. He baffled, however, their most
searching inquiries, and passed the ordeal in
triumph. Then he turned upon his examiners,
gave them questions which they could not
answer, and displayed such wondrous wisdom
and learning that his adversaries were baffled,
and he was declared by acclamation to be his
father's successor.

Solomon was passionately fond of chess,
which he is said to have invented. He was
playing once with his favorite general, Benaiah,
and would have checkmated him as usual, when
just at the critical moment there was a noise in
the street. The king ran to the window to discover the cause of the disturbance, and during
his absence Benaiah took his knight from the
board, and so won the game. Solomon, surprised at the result, as it was the first game
that he had lost, soon concluded that Benaiah
had removed a knight, but said nothing about

it, as he was confident that his general would make a voluntary confession. A day or two afterward he noticed two men acting suspiciously in the street, as if intent on robbery. He quickly assumed a disguise, and hastened out of doors until he met the pair. He assured them that he too was a thief by profession, and promised to admit them to the royal palace, to which he had keys. At nightfall he opened the portals, and led them from room to room until they reached the treasure - chamber. While they were filling their bags with jewels and diamonds, he quietly closed the door, and locked it from without, entrapping them completely. Then he hastened to his own apartment, donned his royal apparel, and summoned his council to conference, Benaiah among the number. When they had assembled, the king asked: "What shall be done to the man who robs his neighbor, and not alone his neighbor but the king himself?" At the words, whose force was intensified by Solomon's glances, which seemed to rest upon him, Benaiah felt certain that the king was referring to his theft at chess. "If I am silent," he said to himself, "until the council decides, I am lost. Confession is the best way to retain the king's favor." Accordingly he rose, humbly confessed his fault, and begged for the royal mercy.

"Ah, my dear general," Solomon replied, with a smile, "I did not assemble the council for thy sake. I have already forgotten, and pardoned thy robbery. There is something else to engage our attention to-day." And then he told them of his adventure with the thieves, who were promptly executed. But Solomon did not so soon forget the contrite confession of his brave general, which he had so cleverly elicited.

RABBINICAL HUMOR.

JUST as in the Talmud the influence of a
double current is visible—the one called
halakhah, the abstract law principle; the other
hagadah, the legend or fanciful tale: so, too,
in the lives of the older rabbis a double influence was clearly at work—the one purely intellectual, impelling men to study the law with
ceaseless diligence; the other more emotional,
springing from a certain moral cheerfulness,
which made them social beings, and preserved
their sense of humor. Their playfulness, indeed, was often a mask assumed to conceal
their real sentiments, and many an innocent
parable must be read between the lines, and
stripped of its hyperbole if its true meaning is
to be gained. As a general rule, however, rabbinical humor is humor unalloyed, designed to
pass away the time, to point a moral, to arouse
the attention, to entertain the children, and

divert the rabbis themselves, and drive home at least one fruitful thought.

A story related of Solomon throws light on the fondness of the rabbis to utter a joke at a wife's expense. Such an act of ungallantry is, happily, fully atoned by many a parable and saying which do ample justice to the virtues of womanhood. It seems that one day Solomon was seated by his palace window, taking a little relaxation from the cares of state, when he noticed two birds on a tree in the garden opposite. The king, as the Bible records, was such a clever philologist as to know even the language of birds, and so he warily listened when the bird addressed its loving mate: " Do you see King Solomon over there, my love ? " " Yes, indeed," was the gentle answer. " Well," said the first speaker, "do you know what I could do, if I wished ? " " No," she rejoined, full of curiosity, " what could you do ? " " Why," he rejoined, with a pompous air, puffing out his wings at full sail, " with one stroke of my wings I could crush every bone in Solomon's body, and with another stroke overturn his palace from turret to foundation-stone."

With proud mien did the mate regard her val-
orous husband, and felt keenly her own femi-
nine insignificance. But Solomon was not
particularly pleased. He summoned the boastful bird to his presence, and angrily asked
what was the meaning of the absurd bragga-
docio he had heard. Then the bird, winking
at the king in shameless style, begged his majesty's pardon. "Of course," said he, "I was
merely joking; I was only fooling my wife—a
husband's privilege, you know. She believes
everything I tell her." And then the little
bird quickly hopped away to his admiring
mate, who is a type of the credulous wife, wor-
shiping her husband as a giant and a hero,
when he possesses not the slightest claims to
greatness.

It is only a few years since a Southern writer
made some interesting contributions to negro
folk-lore, and the figures of Brudder Fox and
Brer Wolf have become familiar to the reading
public. The pranks which the fox played upon
the wolf are by no means so recent as a casual
reader might fancy. They can be traced back
many centuries, and found exemplified in the

folk-lore of various races. It is said, for instance, that one well-known rabbi, Meir, knew three hundred fables about foxes. Here is a fox and wolf story strikingly similar to one of Mr. Harris's tales, and which illustrates, besides, the rabbinical fondness for making even animals recite Biblical verses: A fox once persuaded a wolf to enter a Jewish house, to help prepare the Sabbath meal. No sooner had he crossed the threshold than the entire family set upon him, and he was glad to escape from the blows which were rained upon his head. The wolf was naturally vexed at such treatment; but the fox sought to soothe his ruffled spirit by remarking that probably the wolf's father on another occasion had committed theft in that very dwelling. "What!" the wolf replied, repeating a verse from Ezekiel, "the fathers have eaten sour grapes, and shall the children's teeth be set on edge?" The fox endeavored to reinstate himself in the good opinion of the wolf, and invited the latter to accompany him to a new and more attractive dining-place. He took him to a well, to which two buckets were attached. The fox quickly jumped into the bucket which chanced to be at the top, thereby descending to the well's bottom and raising the other to the surface. When the wolf anxiously inquired why he went down, the fox replied that there was cheese at the bottom, and pointed to the reflection of the moon on the water in proof of his statement. The wolf, all ready for the feast, asked how to descend, and was told to jump into the bucket. Naturally, the other bucket with the fox rose to the top, while the wolf below became conscious of the trick and implored to be raised again. "Ah," said the fox, using a verse from the Proverbs, "'The righteous is delivered out of trouble, and the wicked cometh in his stead.'" Then he added, as a further moral for the wolf to reflect upon, the sentence from Leviticus. "'Just balances and just weights.'"

That the rabbis could be guilty of puns, numerous examples show; but, unfortunately, it is almost impossible to translate their play upon words or give in English an insight into the deft way in which they exercise their humor upon Biblical verses. A fair illustration of such a Biblical pun is the following: On a road through a dense forest stood a solitary inn, whose landlord bore a very unsavory reputation. He was wont to ask each guest his next stopping-place, or the direction of his journey, and at once assert that he intended to take a trip to the same spot, or travel in the same neighborhood, and would be glad to have a companion. Long before dawn he would arouse the traveler, start on the trip, and after they had entered the dark forest, rob him without mercy, or take his life if he offered resistance. Now, one evening a rabbi came to lodge overnight, and at supper, as usual, the landlord asked his customary question. The rabbi stated where he intended to go, and expressed his pleasure at having the landlord as escort. He then retired to rest. At about midnight he was awakened by a violent knocking on the door, and the voice of the landlord calling him to get ready for the journey. "There is time enough," said he. "It is still dark," and he went to sleep again. In an hour or so the landlord knocked once more; but this time the rabbi pleaded his inability to

start until his friend had arrived. "What!" exclaimed the man, not particularly overjoyed, "you expect a friend at this hour! Pray, what is his name?" "My friend's name," the rabbi replied, "is Was-good." The man quickly ran out into the road, calling loudly, "Was-good! Was - good!" but no Mr. Was - good made his appearance. "I don't see your friend," he said, visibly annoyed, as he returned to the inn, and again urged the rabbi to depart. "He must come very soon; he cannot delay much longer," the rabbi answered, enjoying the man's impatience; and after a while he exclaimed in exultant tones, "Why, there he is!" "I don't see him," cried the landlord, mystified. "Look!" the rabbi said, pointing toward the eastern sky, lit up by the first straggling rays of dawn. "There is my friend, the light of day, the best friend of man and beast. Does not the Bible say, 'And God saw the light that it *was-good?*'" In a few moments day had broken in earnest, and the rabbi went on his way rejoicing, while the discomfited landlord pleaded an excuse for not accompanying him.

Much quiet wit is evinced by the rabbis in their replies to skeptics of their day, many of whose objections curiously resemble those raised in our later age. A rabbi was instructing his disciples, when an undevout philosopher entered, and dared him to answer this question: " Who created the world ? " " God," the rabbi replied. " Prove it to me," rejoined the philosopher, "prove it ! " " Come to-morrow, friend," was the answer, " and then I shall adduce the proof." The morrow came, and with it the philosopher. " I'll answer your question," said the rabbi, " if you will first answer mine. Tell me who made the coat you wear ? " " Why, the weaver, of course," was the prompt reply. " The weaver ? " the rabbi repeated. " How do you know that ? Prove it to me." " Why, it stands to reason that the weaver made my coat." " Well," the rabbi rejoined with emphasis, "just as a coat implies a weaver, and a door a carpenter, so the creation implies the Creator, blessed be He ! "

Sometimes the questioner did not receive so kindly a reception. A Persian told the learned Rab that he desired to study Hebrew. " Very well," said the master. "Let us begin at once. This letter is called Aleph." "Aleph?" rejoined the man, incredulous. "How do you prove that it is Aleph?" "This is the second letter, Beth," continued the rabbi. "Beth?" repeated the Persian in the same skeptical tone. "Prove to me that it is Beth." Then Rab became so exasperated that he would not continue the lesson, when the Persian went to the contemporary of Rab, the celebrated Samuel, and applied to him for instruction. He displayed his doubting spirit as before, until Samuel caught him by the ear, and gave it a sharp twinge. "My ear! My ear!" shouted the man in his pain. "Your ear?" repeated Samuel. "Prove to me that it is your ear." "What a strange question!" said the man. "Why, everybody calls it so." "Very true, my friend," was the sage's answer, "and in the same way all call those letters Aleph and Beth. Does this satisfy you?" It is consoling to learn that the Persian became an apt scholar at last, thanks to Samuel's salutary method. Another rabbi gave a more logical answer to a doubter who once thus interrogated him.

"Ye fools who believe in a resurrection! See ye not that the living die? How, then, can ye believe that the dead shall live?" "Foolish man!" the rabbi answered. "Thou believest in a creation? Well, then, if what never before existed exists, why may not that which once existed exist again?" An unbeliever said to Rabbi Gamliel: "When the Bible speaks of the greatness of God, it says that He can tell the number of the stars. What greatness is that? I know their number as well." "Tell me how many teeth thou hast?" said the rabbi in reply. The man put his hand into his mouth to count them. "Thou knowest not what thou hast in thy mouth," the rabbi exclaimed, "and thou pretendest to know the number of the stars?"

Woman, a topic for satire in the sayings and proverbs of every nation, appears of course in the table-talk of the rabbis. Why was Eve formed from Adam's side, and not from another portion of his body? If the head had been selected, she would have been too proud; if the eye, too wanton; if the mouth, too loquacious; if the heart, too passionate; if the hands, too bustling; if the feet, too much of a gada-bout. "A modest side was chosen, that she should be modest," and yet, the rabbis add, woman has a share of all the faults mentioned. When a prince reproached a rabbi for worship-ing a God who practiced theft, seeing that a rib was stolen from Adam, the prince was asked whether he considered it theft if he found a golden cup substituted for a silver one. "But it was done secretly," the prince asserted. "To save Adam from seeing the unpleasant-ness of the process," was the answer. "You would lose your appetite if you saw raw meat in all the stages of being cooked."

Carlyle denies to the Jews any sense of humor: "Hardly any Jew creature, not even a blackguard Heine to any real length," so reads his invective. How little he knew of Semitic humor, which the Hebrews shared in common with their Arab kinsmen! Of humor in its Satanic sense they had nothing; of humor in its genial form, the Talmud is full. It was a standing rule of the rabbis to cultivate cheer-fulness. They recommended, indeed, that teachers shall be especially good-natured in

their intercourse with disciples, and not abrupt-
ly begin the hour of instruction without having
first a little pleasantry. It is distinctly stated
of Rabba, one of the famous masters, that he
used to preface his lessons by humorous anecdotes which put his pupils in a happy frame of
mind. Sometimes an ancedote would be employed to startle an audience, and arouse them
from drowsiness. A rabbi, finding his hearers
rather sleepy, gravely informed them that there
was once a mother in Israel, who had 600,000
children at one birth. Of course, the people
were now wide awake, and when they inquired
as to her name, he answered : " Jochebed."
Certainly the mother of Moses would regard
her son as equal to 600,000 of his brethen.

THE MUNCHAUSEN OF THE
TALMUD.

DURING the early part of the third century of the common era, there lived a rabbi who acquired a national reputation, both in Palestine and Babylonia, as the author of very imaginative stories. These tales survive and stamp him as a Munchausen, centuries before the appearance of that famous baron. But Rabba bar bar Chana—such was the rabbi's name—was more than a mere *raconteur:* he was a scholar and sage besides. Hence there is an added significance in his narratives. They have, in truth, all the delightful flavor of an old salt—they tell of the sea-serpent ages before its regular appearance in the columns of the enterprising daily press. Mr. Rider Haggard's incidents are not to be despised; but they pale into insignificance compared with the marvels on land and sea described by the doughty rab-

bi. Sir John Mandeville is full of wonders,
but Rabba bar bar Chana is his equal. We
are in the atmosphere of the *Arabian Nights;*
the swift-footed Genii are abroad. What mysterious noises, what sudden apparitions, what
fanciful appearances and disappearances ! The
rabbi sedately raises his magic wand, and the
scene changes with the rapidity of a Mephisto.

> " Wandering voices mock the air !
> Forms that phantoms are appear ! "

That numerous commentaries have been
written to explain his sky-rockets of hyperbole,
that his interpreters go to work with the
gravity and resolution of students of Shake-
speare or Goethe, invest his tales with peculiar
interest and assure him a kind of immortality.

Like the proverbial story-teller, there is
nothing bashful about Rabba. What he has
not seen is not worth seeing, and what he has
seen cannot be told in the picturesque strain.
He once saw an Arab transfix a camel with
his lance without disturbing the animal in the
least. The desert of Israel's forty years' wanderings is his favorite camping-ground. An

Arab shows him Mount Sinai, and he hears from its summit a divine voice: " Woe that I have sworn! and now after I have sworn to exile Israel from his land—who will release me from the oath ? " He sees the very spot where Korah and his followers were swallowed up, and from the smoking depths these words are borne to his receptive ears, " Moses is truth, and his law is truth ; but we are liars." He views the exact spot where heaven and earth kiss each other. He hung his bread-basket there and went away, but when he returned, his basket was not to be found. His guide told him that if he would revisit the place in twenty-four hours, he would find the basket once more—could the earth's rotation be illustrated in a more poetic parable ?

The sea-stories that Rabba so cheerfully and constantly spun in days when the sea was shrouded in much more mystery than now, bear the mark of the traditional traveler. " I once was at sea," so he sagely relates, " and there I saw a fish whose back was covered with sand and grass. We all thought it was an island and landed, starting a fire to cook our food. But when the fish felt the warmth, it turned over, and we would have been drowned if a ship had not rescued us." Upon another occasion, Rabba saw a bird which stood to its lower joints in the water, while its head reached the sky. He and his friends thought that the sea must here be shallow, and they prepared without any hesitation to bathe, when a voice exclaimed : " Enter not the water. A carpenter, seven years ago, let fall his axe on this very spot, and it has not yet touched bottom : not that the water is deep, but its current is rapid."

Could a fish story of modern date equal the following ? Rabba was once at sea when an immense fish was sighted. A small insect crept into its nose and caused its death. The waves cast ashore the body, which in its onset destroyed sixty cities. Its flesh nourished sixty cities more, while enough nutriment was left to serve as salt-fish for sixty other cities. Three hundred measures of oil streamed from its eyes. After the lapse of a few years, Rabba visited the place again, and found that the sixty destroyed cities had been rebuilt from its

bones.   It was not enough, however, for Rabba
to tell about a huge fish.   He once saw an
enormous frog, as large as sixty houses.   It
was swallowed at one gulp by a serpent, which
in its turn was digested by a sea-monster.
After the full meal, the fish coolly sat upon a
tree.   How strong a tree that must have been!
" If I had not been present," adds another sage,
" I would not have believed it."   Did the ex-
aggeration exhaust Rabba?   Not at all.   His
vessel was once carried aloft by a tremendous
wave, so close to a star that the people on
board were almost scorched by the stellar
heat.

It is possible that many of Rabba's tales
were but

> " The children of an idle brain
> Begot of nothing but vain fantasy;"

yet some bear the mark of earnest purpose.
They were parables for the times, sermons for
the people, and couched in a style that would
emphasize the truth which was sought to be
conveyed.   When he told of the sea-monster
which was mistaken for land, until it turned
over and threatened them with destruction,

may he not have hinted at the Roman power,
which apparently gave shelter, only at last to
overwhelm them ? In those troublous ages,
with informers and sycophants at every step,
political topics could be discussed only in a
guarded way ; and the witty hyperbole was a
mask for teaching many a home truth, which
the people could readily understand and apply
to their own condition. The moral beauty in
many of Rabba's stories is not to be denied,
and their interpretation is a favorite with old-
time preachers. Could duty to the dead be
more powerfully exemplified than in the following incident ? Rabba relates that, while
traveling in the wilderness, he came upon dead
bodies of immense size, with their faces up-
turned to the sky. He sprang from his camel
and took the fringe from the garment of one of
them. He remounted the animal, but it refused to advance a step until he had restored
the stolen fringe.

More lovely and suggestive is the story of
the golden dove, which proves that Rabba was
more than a mere humorist and satirist. He was
traveling once with a caravan, and was resum-

ing the journey after a rest for dinner, when he
became suddenly aware of the fact that he had
forgotten to say the customary blessing after
meals. He wished to repeat the prescribed
prayer at the spot where he had eaten, but did
not desire to acquaint his companions with the
fact because they would not recognize the pro-
priety of the law. So he gave as an excuse,
that he had forgotten the golden figure of a
dove, and wished to return. He started back,
reached the spot of the previous station, uttered
the prayer, and found in truth a golden dove.
Could fantasy suggest a more striking parable
to illustrate the worth of religious precepts ?

One of the most obscure and enigmatic of
Rabba's sayings has received such a serious
and elaborate interpretation that it may be
properly given here. "I was traveling in the
desert," Rabba observes, "when I noticed a
flock of geese, whose feathers had fallen off by
reason of their fatness, and the fat was flowing
from under them like a stream. I said to them:
'Will any of you have a portion in the future
world ?' Upon this, one of them uplifted a
leg, and another its wing. When I told this to

Rabbi Eleazar, he said to me, ' Israel will some day have to give an account for this.' " The interpretation is as follows : The fatness of the goose is the symbol of stupidity and ignorance. The wing represents the loftiness of wisdom, signifying in this allegory the mind, which possesses great capacities that are often neglected and hence sink into sensuality. It was Rabba's purpose to state that during his journey of life he had found people of great ability, whose intellect was burdened by too many worldly duties, and who were led away by the gratifications of earth. Astounded at their neglect of mental culture, he examined this class of men as to whether they knew anything about another and a better existence— the world of knowledge and learning. Thereupon, one of them pointed to his well-fed body, expressing the thought that bodily pleasure alone was his idea of happiness, intellectual and spiritual life being unknown to him. Another, however, showed him his wing, and Rabba inferred from this action that they were still capable of the intellectual enjoyments of that other world, after which he was so diligently inquiring. When he had related his experiences to Rabbi Eleazar, the latter said : "For those who have mental powers and abilities which they willfully neglect, in their entire abandonment to earthly gains and pursuits, Israel will have, one day, to give solemn and strict account before God."

THE RABBI'S DREAM.

IF ever poverty had fastened upon a dwelling, it was in the humble abode of Hanina. The scholars of his time were rarely noted for their opulence — they were satisfied to maintain themselves by honest toil, and never lost heart, however heavily the cares of life pressed upon them. In Hanina's case the shadows were dark indeed; but he was not the man to murmur. A little was ample for himself and family. Their wants were few and readily supplied if water and bread were forthcoming.

Yet Hanina was no ordinary sage. Modest, unassuming, and always content, like a bird, if a few crumbs fell to his share, he was regarded as possessing marvelous gifts and the ability to perform miracles. Poor Hanina! was not existence itself a miracle amid thy surroundings? Was there not something super-

natural in thy self-control and contentment, in
the warmth of thy faith in the Eternal goodness, although thy hearthstone was cold and
bare? Surely there must have been a miracle-
working power in that soul of thine which kept
thy countenance so placid and uncomplaining.
What angelic agencies must have accompanied
thee on thy walk to the academy and kept
watch over thee in the debates and discussions
of the masters! Otherwise how couldst thou
have displayed such learning and skill, with
hunger and want gnawing within thee? The
good man, already crowned with the gift of
divination, kept straight to the path assigned
him and seemed to the outer world lost in philosophic thought. But his wife was far from
being a prophet. She was intensely a woman,
and however ardently she loved her husband,
she desired no martyrdom. The cold blast
could not be philosophized away. The children's hunger and her own necessities were
facts ever present to her, and she felt that
life was unduly hard. She grew ashamed of
her poverty, which seemed to become greater
and greater, and strove to conceal it as far as

possible from her inquisitive neighbors. She
saved, she toiled, and she was abundantly content if once a week she could throw a blazing
log into the oven, spreading a pillar of smoke
which made it appear as if the weekly portion
of bread was being baked. The deceit was
pardonable, and it escaped detection for a time.

In the neighborhood there lived a rather
malicious woman who despised Hanina and his
family for their poverty, and who could not
understand the weekly volumes of smoke issu-
ing from their wretched abode. "What a sub-
terfuge!" she exclaimed to herself at last.
"But they cannot deceive me. The trick is
too transparent. I know they have no flour.
How, then, can they bake bread? I'll tear
away their mas!—the beggars that they are!"

Full of wrath, which is often called righteous
according to the point of view, she hastened
to Hanina's dwelling one day when the rising
smoke was no longer to be endured, so obnox-
ious had the sham become. She knocked at
the door sharply and vigorously, as though
she had an important duty to discharge which
would brook no delay. Hanina's wife was

within and trembled at the sound. Visitors were rare and were certainly least welcome at that moment. With throbbing heart she opened the door, and, recognizing her visitor and the purpose of the visit, she blushed and fled into another room, leaving the field clear for the enemy.

The visitor was all smiles. No opportunity could be more propitious. She was mistress of all she surveyed. With a bound she rushed to the oven and peered within. Oh, marvel of marvels ! It was full of bread, full to repletion. In her surprise and confusion she shouted: "Come, neighbor, be quick ! The shovel ! The bread is burning !" Hanina's wife hurried into the room, concealed her amazement, and saved the bread from destruction. Thus had the Lord performed a miracle to prevent Hanina's wife being put to shame.

It was evening. Hanina came home and was met at the threshold by the wife. The wonderful story was quickly told. He listened, but said nothing. Silence is often of the highest wisdom.

" Dear husband," said his wife, after a pause.

"I have something more to say to thee. Nay, be not angry. I can no longer hold my peace. Tell me truly. Dost thou think that we shall forever lead such a life as is ours? Will poverty be always our lot? Are we never to enjoy a little sunshine, a little prosperity? Must our helpless children become beggars like their parents?"

"I am not angry, dear wife," the husband answered. "I know thy hardships, but I share them as well. What can I do?"

"What canst thou do!" the woman repeated, half in anger, half in derision—"What canst thou do! Art thou not a worker of miracles? Do not thy prayers cure the sick and restore to life the dying? Pray, then, for thine own. Let thy wife and children have some happiness in this world—a little more warmth and food and raiment than they now possess. Surely in the world to come there is a large share of wealth for so good and learned a man as thou art. Why not pray to God to allow thee some portion of it, however small, in our present existence?"

What could the poor man do? Entreated so earnestly by his wife, he withstood her im-

portunities for a while, for he thought them
unworthy and irreligious. But when he found
that he could pacify her in no other way, he
resigned himself to his lot and began to pray.
Gentle at first were his tones of prayer, and
ever gentler, until only his lips moved, framing
the thoughts that sprang from his heart. While
he was thus ardently praying, his eyes up-
raised, his hands extended, he saw something
shining in the distance and descending slowly.
Fancy his astonishment when, as if in answer
to his petition, there fell at his feet a massive
golden leg of a golden table.

What were Hanina's emotions as he raised
his treasure ! He trembled and almost wept.
And he felt self-accused, as though he had
committed a crime. His conscience smote him,
he knew not why. He went to bed, but could
not sleep, so active was his fantasy. A thousand forms danced before him. A thousand
aspects of cloud and mist pursued him in the
visions of the night. And then he slept, while
a deep, mysterious dream fell upon him.

He stood before the gates of Heaven, whose
portals swung open to receive him. The heav-

enly abode was all ablaze with gold and jewels, while the departed sat at their heavenly meal, each at a splendid golden table of his own. He, too, seemed to be seated before a table; but it shook and trembled, and when he tried to steady it, he found his labor in vain. A leg was missing.

Terrified, the man awoke. The full significance of the dream burst upon him. It was a warning which he dared not neglect. Was he to imperil future happiness by pleasure that was as transitory as the mist and as little real? When the holy ones of all races and creeds were enjoying future bliss, was he alone to be unsatisfied, agitated by the consciousness of guilt?

" Take thy gift back, O God!" Hanina cried in his agony. " Take it back and restore me my peace of soul!"

The gift vanished as mysteriously as it appeared, and Hanina never told his dream. He felt more firmly than ever the truth in the saying of the sages that no man can enjoy two meals—the one on earth, the other in heaven.

THE GIFT THAT BLESSED.

FEW men were better known than Aben
Judan. It was not only his wealth which
spread his name and fame, but his unfailing
benevolence and the courtesies which he extended to all. He was the earliest to respond
to the call of charity, and his personal services
as well as his gold were alike at the disposal
of the people. It is not surprising, then, that
they loved him more and more, and the rabbis
who annually traveled through Palestine to
collect funds in aid of the poor, knew in advance who would be their most generous con-
tributor. Yet all the splendor of fortune did
not dazzle Aben Judan: he retained a certain
modesty of disposition and simplicity of character; and his faith was childlike and un-
questioning.

The day arrived, however, when Aben Judan

was to learn that earthly wealth had no permanence. A succession of calamities overwhelmed the province in which he lived. First,
the storm-wind raged with fearful violence,
destroying his luxuriant crops, uprooting his
sturdy trees, and demolishing his buildings.
His fair estate was a prey to the hurricane's
devastation, and nought escaped. Then, perhaps as a result of the widespread ruin which
drove his flocks and herds from their accustomed pastures, a distemper broke out among
the cattle. It could not be checked, it rapidly
gained headway, and soon Aben Judan, who
surely did not deserve these hard strokes of
fate, lost the greater part of his property. His
land alone remained, which was quickly seized
by creditors to meet their own obligations in
the general panic.

The reverse of fortune was complete and
terrific. It would have prostrated a man of
less heroic build; but Aben Judan, though he
bent to the blow, preserved his equanimity,
and was far from being utterly cast down. He
had health yet—he could begin anew; such
changes were part of life's varied experiences;

he could meet them manfully, and, like Job, declare, " The Lord gave, and the Lord hath taken away; blessed be the name of the Lord ! "

With this benediction on his lips, and his heart all aglow with gratitude, even at the moment of his apparent wretchedness, he retired to a small cabin and cultivated a remnant of land which was happily rescued from the general wreck. So diligently did he labor, his olden activity and intelligence coming to his aid, that his work was blessed beyond his most sanguine hopes. He was enabled to maintain his own family—that was his first ambition—and then how happy was he to find that he could also relieve the distress of others ! His lowly cabin formed the strongest possible contrast to his stately residence in the past; but his heart retained its old-time charity, and he was comforted.

It chanced one evening, as he was resting before the door after the fatigues of the day, and talking cheerfully to his children, who surrounded him, the news was brought that the three rabbis, who were accustomed to pay annual visits to the neighborhood, were on their rounds again, and might be expected at any moment. A change fell upon Aben Judan: he could not control his emotion. He became pale and agitated, and withdrew from the circle of children with an exclamation of despair.

"What ails thee, dear husband?" his wife tenderly inquired; for she had noticed his sudden sadness, and had followed him within. "Has some illness befallen thee which thou seekest to conceal? What is thy trouble?"

"I have no illness," he replied, after a brief pause. "Yet my trouble is grievous, and would to heaven thou couldst assuage it. But that is impossible. It is God alone who can help at this crisis. Dost thou remember, wife, in the days of our prosperity how we rejoiced to aid the destitute? Our corn fed the hungry, our wool clothed the naked, and our wine cheered the sad at heart. What times were those! How the orphans blessed us, the widows shed tears of joy at our approach, what happiness we diffused, which returned to us an hundredfold! What bliss it was to participate in kindly deeds and realize the delight of scattering love to the deserving poor! But all that is now changed. We cannot aid others, because we ourselves are so wretched and needy."

"Why, husband, thy words surprise me!" the wife exclaimed, deeply moved. "Thou art usually so happy in thy disposition, and dost never murmur against the will of God. Why art thou now so discontented?"

"Didst thou not hear," Aben Judan answered, "didst thou not hear that the collectors are coming? What sums we used to give them, what bounty gladdened them in the past! What have we now to offer?"

"Is this the cause of thy distress?" the wife replied. "God has not left thee destitute. Thou hast still some means. Hast thou not this very field? Let us sell one-half of it and give the proceeds to the rabbis. There, beloved husband, canst thou be disconsolate now?"

At her words Aben Judan's countenance beamed with joy. His old energy returned to him, his gloom departed.

"Dearest," he cried, "thou hast made me happy again. My heart can safely confide in thee."

Without delay Aben Judan followed his

wife's suggestion, and sold half of his field. When the rabbis came he gave them the sum he had received, which they gratefully accepted, and on taking their leave they said, as a parting benediction: "May the Lord restore to thee all thy wealth. Thine is the gift which blesses!"

Was it the hope which these words inspired? Was it the consciousness of duty done? From the moment he began to work on the little ground remaining to him, his spirits rose, his industry was unflagging, he knew neither pain nor anxiety. And his wife encouraged him at his toil—she had murmured a devout "Amen!" when the rabbis blessed her husband, and she felt confident that their farewell words would be realized.

One day, while Aben Judan was tilling his field with his ox, the animal's forefeet suddenly sank in an excavation. Had another misfortune happened? Was he about to lose the only ox he possessed? In haste he unyoked the poor beast, and managed to extricate him from the hole, but when he examined it more closely he saw something shining far below.

He resolved to descend, and enlarged the excavation, when what was his amazement at finding an immense treasure, which one of his ancestors had deposited in troublous times.

With throbbing heart he conveyed the treasure to his home. At the threshold he told his wife, amid her tears of joy, what had occurred. Soon he was enabled to repurchase his former possessions, and became again the generous friend of the poor and unfortunate.

The months passed, and the period again arrived for the rabbis to visit the district on their charitable rounds. They approached the cabin where Aben Judan had lived when they had last met him, but found him not. So they inquired of the villagers as to his place of residence.

" Aben Judan ! " they rejoined, "why, who can equal him in goodness and wealth ? Do ye see those flocks ? They are his. Do ye mark those far-extending fields, those vineyards and gardens so magnificent, those splendid buildings ? All, all belong to him, our benefactor."

In a moment Aben Judan drew near and

greeted the rabbis in his cordial way; they returned his salutations as warmly.

" Well, dear friends," he exclaimed, " your wishes and prayers have been heard, and abundantly fulfilled. Come now with me, and receive a portion of the blessing ye bestowed upon me. I shall try to make full compensation for the small subscription of the past year."

The rabbis followed him to his new abode, which was more spacious than his dwelling in his early days of good fortune, and there they were greeted by his wife, and well entertained. On parting, Aben Judan gave them a present for the poor larger than he had ever contributed before.

" Have I made amends," he asked, " for last year's humble offering ? "

" We have a secret to tell thee," one of the rabbis answered. " Here is a list of last year's gifts, and, although many gave larger sums, thine is placed at the head. We knew that thy poverty, not thy soul, made the amount small. And yet it was thy gift which blessed."

" Praise me not, dear friends," Aben Judan replied. " Does it not say in Holy Writ, ' Thou shalt not appear before the Eternal with empty hands. According as the Lord thy God has blessed thee, shalt thou give to the poor.' "

IN THE SWEAT OF THY BROW.

THE spirit of the Talmud is the spirit of work and worship. Both were insisted upon: pickaxe as well as psalm. The early settlers in New England, who sowed their corn with one eye on their implement of husbandry and the other on the implement of war; Cromwell's men, who consulted their prayer-books as often as their muskets—these were kindred in character to the olden rabbis. They could fight, could sow, could weave, could mend sails or shoes, and were adepts in every variety of trade and handiwork, and could join just as stoutly in prayer and benediction, in earnest study and profound research. They were trained in a capital school—that of human experience; and if reading, travel, observation, suffering, did not sharpen their sagacity, many were hereditary artificers, men and women whose sires had developed their taste and skill in connection with the building and furnishing of the Tabernacle and Temple. They were no nerveless ecclesiastics or pious weaklings. Their atmosphere was that of the workshop, not of the confessional. The synagogue was a school and assembly as well as prayer-meeting.

The proverb is the mirror of a nation's thought, and reflects unerringly the national trait and custom. Rabbinical sayings prove that the rabbis regarded all work as sacred. They preached the holiness of labor ages before Carlyle, and with more sincerity, for he labored with his pen alone; but they took part in the conflicts of history, fought and labored as well as thought and studied. As in " The Courtship of Miles Standish," it could be said of them: " You are a writer and I am a fighter, but here is a fellow who could both write and fight, and in both was equally skillful."

It is a saying of Rabbi Joshua ben Levi that when God spoke to Adam the words, " Thorns and thistles will grow for you," tears gushed from his eyes, and he said, " Shall I then eat with my ass from one crib?" Quickly God replied, "In the sweat of thy countenance shalt thou eat bread." Then Adam was soothed. His soul was comforted in its affliction. He saw in labor compensation and consolation for life's bitterness and sin. The earth might be cursed for his disobedience, but the fruits of his industry would sweeten the struggle for existence. "Cover dead cattle on the public road and take thy pay and think not, 'I am a great man or priest, and the work is despicable to me'"—so reads a passage in the Talmud. No work is to be despised if it saves one from mendicancy. "Great is labor," runs another Talmudic saying, "for it honors its master." "God did not permit His glory to rest upon Israel," says Rabbi Tarphon, "until it had accomplished a work." It is stated (Ex. xxv. 8), "Ye shall erect me a sanctuary, and *then* I shall dwell in your midst." "If there are seven years of famine," reads another rabbinical saying, "it enters not the laborer's and artisan's door."

Once a certain Simeon, a man of some capacity, who dug cisterns and wells for a liveli-

hood, accosted Johanan ben Sakkai with the
unflattering remark: " I am as great as thou."
"How so?" rejoined the rabbi, somewhat
amused. " Because I busy myself as much as
thou dost with the necessities of the commu-
nity. For instance," he continued, " if any one
comes to thee to consult upon some legal or
religious question, thou sayest, ' Drink from
this well, for its waters are pure and cold. . . .'"
Simeon's logic was clear and unanswerable.
If the well and the bath had not been constructed, how could the rabbi's commands be
executed? Hence the artisan is as necessary
as the sage for the observance of the law, and
must be placed upon the same moral plane.

Although the rabbis say, " Who teaches no
trade to his son teaches him to steal," different
views obtained among them on the question
of uniting study and labor. The general eth-
ical principle was laid down that not theory
but practice was the chief requisite, as they
wished to guard against hypocrisy and formal-
ism. But it was held by some, for example
Simon ben Jochai, that heavy manual labor
might be performed by slaves, so as to allow

Israelites more time for study. Ishmael took the opposite view. He interpreted the passage, " Thou shalt gather thy grain" (Deut. xi. 14), to mean that study and manual labor were to be united, each in its own time and manner. Rabbi Ishmael gained the day; his explanation found acceptance; and those who acted as he did, the Talmud further relates, succeeded, while those who acted as Simon ben Jochai, failed.

There was abundant reason for the remark of Rabbi Nehorai : " I let go all the employments in the universe and teach my son nothing but the law." He did not mean, perhaps, to despise useful labor, but desired rather to express his reverence for the Law, to which Israel owed so much, and in whose study it forgot every privation and suffering. His colleagues, however, were wiser and not less reverent when they placed law and labor on the same level, in the beautiful thought which has been handed down by the sages of Jamnia : " I am a creature of God and my neighbor the same; my work is in the city, his in the field. I rise early to my work, and he rises early to his. As he does not boast of his work, I do not boast of mine. If you think I achieve much and he little, we have learned, 'One who achieves little is as one who achieves much, if only his heart be heavenward!'" Not a bad text that for translation into life! It reminds one of Tennyson's Sir Galahad, whose work prospered because his heart was pure.

The older rabbis not only preached the blessings of industry, but they belonged largely to the industrial classes. The spirit of their teachings is aptly illustrated in the incident told of Abnemos, the weaver, who asked Abba Joseph, an architect, a religious question, just as the latter was engaged in the scaffolding of a balcony. But Abba Joseph refused to descend and waste his time in idle discussion, as he was a day laborer. Joshua ben Hananya, one of the most famous of his generation, was one day visited by Gamaliel, who wished to be reconciled to him, as they had exchanged words on a question of law. When Gamaliel entered, he exclaimed : "From the walls of thy house, blackened and dust-covered, men can tell that thou art a blacksmith." Joshua, fancying that

Gamaliel, who was a rabbi of great wealth, had come to mock his lowly occupation, replied with considerable heat: " Woe to the generation whose leader thou art! woe to the ship whose helmsman thou art! for thou knowest not the poverty of the scholars and in what anxiety they live." As little ashamed of his trade was the son of Illai, who used to carry into the school-house the cask he made—he was a cooper—and seated upon it gave instructions to his pupils.

Varied indeed were the occupations of the rabbis of the Talmud. Bar Adah was a surveyor; the illustrious Hillel was a woodsplitter. Agriculture was a favorite with many. There were shoemakers not a few, and tailors, bakers, basketmakers, carpenters, cattle-dealers, millers, dyers, in good numbers; Abba Saul was latterly a grave-digger, but at first a wine-dealer. He was so conscientious in trade that he did not wish to retain the lees in a cask, which, he claimed, belonged to the purchaser. He collected a large quantity and brought it to the Temple treasurers in Jerusalem. Although they accounted the lees as his property, he would make no use of it. Upon his death-bed he would stretch forth his hand and exclaim, "This hand was righteous in measuring." When Huna was asked to act as judge, he said, "Get a man who will draw water in my stead and I will act as judge." He was a poor farmer, and once, returning from his little plot of ground, with spade on his shoulder, he was met by the wealthy Hama, who wished to carry the spade. But Huna would not allow it, and continued on his way unconcerned. Hassda was a brewer, and grew so wealthy that he built an academy at Sura.

Certain occupations were looked upon with disfavor, if not directly prohibited: donkey and camel-drivers, sailors, mud-collectors, petty merchants and shepherds. Trades, such as those of weavers, perfumers, tanners, bathers, washers, and wool-carders, were not supposed to add to one's reputation. It was Judah the Holy—the only one among the rabbis to receive the title—who said: "There is no trade which will disappear from the world; happy is he who has seen practiced by his parents a beautiful and respected trade; and happy is he who has inherited no disreputable occupation."

Rabbi Meir taught: "One should strive to teach his son an easy and cleanly industry. Let us pray to Him to whom belong wealth and goods, for in every trade there is as much wealth as poverty. But neither poverty nor wealth depends upon the work; far more they depend upon the worth and merit of the worker."

Although trade-guilds, in the modern sense, did not exist in Talmudic times, a spirit of association prevailed. Certain occupations in connection with the Temple service were hereditary, and the authorities had to tolerate the monopoly; as the workmen they once brought from Alexandria for the purpose were found unskillful and they had to double the wages of the original artisans. The coppersmiths had a separate synagogue and cemetery in Jerusalem. Insurance companies flourished. In the great synagogue at Alexandria, famous for its size and splendor, the various trades were grouped together— gold, silver, copper, and blacksmiths and weavers. When a poor man entered, the Talmud distinctly states, he recognized his fellow-workmen and turned to them, receiving food for himself and family.

The rabbis were so deeply imbued with the necessity of work that in their views of the Deity they regarded Him as a master-mechanic or employer. "The day is short," so reads one of their familiar sayings, "the work much, the workmen lazy, the reward great, and the Master urgent. Yet not like slaves are we to work, in the hope of reward. We are to work rather for work's sake alone, with the fear of Heaven upon us; that is, with reverence for the Deity." This was the rabbinical ideal in those distant centuries; thus did they labor, taking no pay for their services as teachers of the congregation. They taught what they wanted the people to know, not what the people wanted them to say.

A FOUR-LEAVED CLOVER.

I.

GREAT was the alarm in the palace of Rome, which soon spread throughout the entire city. The Empress had lost her costly diadem, and it could not be found. They searched in every direction, but it was all in vain. Half distracted, for the mishap boded no good to her or her house, the Empress redoubled her exertions to regain her precious possession, but without result. As a last resource it was proclaimed in the public streets : "The Empress has lost a priceless diadem. Whoever restores it within thirty days shall receive a princely reward. But he who delays, and brings it after thirty days, shall lose his head."

In those times all nationalities flocked toward Rome; all classes and creeds could be met in its stately halls and crowded thorough-fares. Among the rest was a rabbi, a learned sage from the East, who loved goodness, and lived a righteous life, in the stir and turmoil of the Western world. It chanced one night as he was strolling up and down, in busy medita-tion, beneath the clear, moonlit sky, he saw the diadem sparkling at his feet. He seized it quickly, brought it to his dwelling, where he guarded it carefully until the thirty days had expired, when he resolved to return it to the owner.

He proceeded to the palace, and, undismayed at sight of long lines of soldiery and officials, asked for an audience with the Empress.

"What dost thou mean by this?" she in-quired, when he told her his story and gave her the diadem. "Why didst thou delay un-til this hour? Dost thou know the penalty? Thy head must be forfeited."

"I delayed until now," the rabbi answered calmly, "so that thou mightst know that I return thy diadem, not for the sake of the re-ward, still less out of fear of punishment; but solely to comply with the Divine command not to withhold from another the property which belongs to him."

" Blessed be thy God!" the Empress answered, and dismissed the rabbi without further reproof; for had he not done right for right's sake?

II.

A certain father was doubly blessed—he had reached a good old age, and had ten sons. One day he called them to his side, and after repeated expressions of affection, told them that he had acquired a fortune by industry and economy, and would give them one hundred gold pieces each before his death, so that they might begin business for themselves, and not be obliged to wait until he had passed away. It happened, however, that, soon after, he lost a portion of his property, much to his regret, and had only nine hundred and fifty gold pieces left. So he gave one hundred to each of his nine sons. When his youngest son, whom he loved most of all, asked naturally what was to be his share, the father replied:

" My son, I promised to give each of thy

brothers one hundred gold pieces. I shall keep my word to them. I have fifty left. Thirty I shall reserve for my funeral expenses, and twenty will be thy portion. But understand this—I possess, in addition, ten friends, whom I give over to thee as compensation for the loss of the eighty gold pieces. Believe me, they are worth more than all the gold and silver."

The youth tenderly embraced his parent, and assured him that he was content, such was his confidence and affection. In a few days the father died, and the nine sons took their money, and without a thought of their youngest brother, and the small amount he had received, followed each his own fancy. But the youngest son, although his portion was the least, resolved to heed his father's words, and hold fast to the ten friends. When a short time had elapsed he prepared a simple feast, went to the ten friends of his father, and said to them: " My father, almost in his last words, asked me to keep you, his friends, in honor. Before I leave this place to seek my fortune elsewhere, will you not share with me a farewell meal, and aid me thus to comply with his dying request ? "

The ten friends, stirred by his earnestness and cordiality, accepted his invitation with pleasure, and enjoyed the repast, although they were used to richer fare. When the moment for parting arrived, however, one of them rose and spoke : " My friends, it seems to me that of all the sons of our dear friend that has gone, the youngest alone is mindful of his father's friendship for us, and reverences his memory. Let us, then, be true friends to him, for his own sake as well, and provide for him a generous sum, that he may begin business here, and not be forced to live among strangers."

The proposal, so unexpected and yet so merited, was received with applause. The youth, proud of their friendship, soon became a prosperous merchant, who never forgot that faithful friends were more valuable than gold or silver, and left an honored name to his descendants.

III.

There lived once a very wealthy man, who cared little for money, except as a means for helping others. He used to adopt a peculiar plan in his method of charitable relief. He had three boxes made for the three different classes of people whom he desired to assist. In one box he put gold pieces, which he distributed among artists and scholars, for he honored knowledge and learning as the highest possession. In the second box he placed silver pieces for widows and orphans, for whom his sympathies were readily awakened. In the third were copper coins for the general poor and beggars—no one was turned away from his dwelling without some gift, however small.

That the man was beloved by all, need hardly be said. He rejoiced that he was enabled to do so much good, retained his modest bearing, and continued to regard his wealth as only an incentive to promote the happiness of mankind, without distinction of creed or nationality. Unhappily, his wife was just the opposite. She rarely gave food or raiment to the poor, and felt angry at her husband's liberality, which she considered shameless extravagance.

The day came when in the pressure of various duties he had to leave his house, and could not return until the morrow. Unaware of his sudden departure, the poor knocked at the door as usual for his kind gifts; but when they found him absent, they were about to go away or remain in the street, being terrified at the thought of asking his wife for alms. Vexed at their conduct, she exclaimed impetuously: "I will give to the poor according to my husband's method."

She seized the keys of the boxes, and first opened the box of gold. But how great was her terror when she gazed at its contents—frogs jumping here and there. Then she went to the silver box, and it was full of ants. With troubled heart, she opened the copper box, and it was crowded with creeping bugs. Loud then were her complaints, and bitter her tears, at the deception, and she kept her room until her husband returned.

No sooner did the man enter the room, annoyed that so many poor people were kept waiting outside, than she asked him: "Why did you give me keys to boxes of frogs, ants, and bugs, instead of gold, silver, and copper?

Was it right thus to deceive your wife, and dis-
appoint the poor ? "

" Not so," rejoined her husband. " The mis-
take must be yours, not mine. I have given
you the right keys. I do not know what you
have done with them. Come, let me have
them. I am guiltless of any deception." He
took the keys, quickly opened the boxes, and
found the coins as he had left them. " Ah,
dear wife," said he, when she had regained
her composure, "your heart, I fear, was not
in the gift, when you wished to give to the poor.
It is the feeling that prompts us to aid, not the
mere money, which is the chief thing after all."

And ever after her heart was changed. Her
gifts blessed the poor of the land, and aroused
their love and reverence.

IV.

In an Eastern city a lovely garden flourished, whose beauty and luxuriance awakened
much admiration. It was the owner's greatest
pleasure to watch its growth, as leaf, flower,
and tree seemed daily to unfold to brighter
bloom. One morning, while taking his usual

stroll through the well-kept paths, he was surprised to find that some blossoms were picked
to pieces. The next day he noticed more signs
of mischief, and rendered thus more observant
he gave himself no rest until he had discovered
the culprit. It was a little trembling bird,
whom he managed to capture, and was about
to kill in his anger, when it exclaimed: "Do
not kill me, I beg you, kind sir. I am only a
wee, tiny bird. My flesh is too little to satisfy
you. I would not furnish one-hundredth of a
meal to a man of your size. Let me free without any hesitation, and I shall teach you something that will be of much use to you and your
friends."

"I would dearly like to put an end to you,"
replied the man, "for you were rapidly putting
an end to my garden. It is a good thing to rid
the world of such annoyances. But as I am
not revengeful, and am always glad to learn
something useful, I shall set you free this time."
And he opened his hand to give the bird more
air.

"Attention!" cried the bird. "Here are
three rules which should guide you through

life, and if you observe them you will find your path made easier: Do not cry over spilt milk; do not desire what is unattainable, and do not believe what is impossible."

The man was satisfied with the advice, and let the bird escape; but it had scarcely regained its liberty, when, from a high tree opposite, it exclaimed:

"What a silly man! The idea of letting me escape! If you only knew what you have lost! But it is too late now."

"What have I lost?" the man asked, angrily.

"Why, if you had killed me, as you intended, you would have found inside of me a huge pearl, as large as a goose's egg, and you would have been a wealthy man forever."

"Dear little bird," the man said in his blandest tones; "sweet little bird, I will not harm you. Only come down to me, and I will treat you as if you were my own child, and give you fruit and flowers all day. I assure you of this most sacredly."

But the bird shook its head sagely, and replied: "What a silly man, to forget so soon the advice which was given him in all seriousness. I told you not to cry over spilt milk, and here you are, worrying over what has happened. I urged you not to desire the unattainable, and now you wish to capture me again. And, finally, I asked you not to believe what is impossible, and you are rashly imagining that I have a huge pearl inside of me, when a goose's egg is larger than my whole body. You ought to learn your lessons better in the future, if you would become wise," added the bird, as with another twist of its head it flew away, and was lost in the distance.

THE EXPIATION.

IT was a happy, buoyant maiden who was
rapidly walking along the fragrant country paths on some errand for her parents, perhaps, or merely for the exercise in the pleasant
afternoon air. Bright visions must have danced
across her fancy, for her eyes were shining,
and she laughed repeatedly in the gladsome
unconsciousness of youth and health.

"How thirsty I am!" she said to herself,
pausing for a moment, and gazing around. "If
I only had a cooling draught of water! Why,
there is a well! How fortunate, indeed! I
shall take a few mouthfuls anyway, and rest
awhile in the shade. It looks so inviting there."

She hastened to the well by the wayside—
an everlasting boon to the traveler in the Orient—and stooped over in her eagerness, hold-
ing on to the branch of a tree, which stood

sentinel on the spot. Suddenly it snapped under the pressure, and the girl was precipitated below. Happily, the broken bough, which fell with her, saved her from instant death; for it became wedged in the well, and gave her a slight foothold just above the surface of the water.

When she recovered consciousness from the shock of the fall, the afternoon had faded into eve, and the few stars that glittered above her head told her that night was rapidly approaching. The merriment had forsaken her now— her smiles and laughter belonged to the remote past. Her thoughts were of her home and her parents, the general anxiety that would be felt at her sudden disappearance, and the abrupt ending of her young life. What had she done to deserve so sad a fate? Was it because she had been too happy? But perhaps her absence would be discovered, and people would search for her, and find her at last. Regaining her courage, after a silent prayer, her voice broke the stillness, and her appeals for help, shouted with all her young strength, were reëchoed again and again. Then she waited for some response, but nothing seemed to stir, save the birds which darted across the well, and the trees which swayed to and fro. No intelligible sound came to her but the echo of her voice, which she hardly recognized at first, so despairing was its tone. Her anxious heart-beats came loud and fast. Soon the stars shone out still more clearly, as if midnight were at hand, and the songs of the dawn were next to be heard. How endless was the weary waiting! She resigned herself to the inevitable—the branch at her feet seemed to be giving way, and she was slipping slowly to her fate. There was no hope. The end had come. Again her voice rang out in her despair.

"Who's there?" came a cry from above.

"Save me, save me!" shouted the maiden in response, while new hope gave strength to her utterance. "Save me! I am down in the well. Be quick! My support is giving way."

In a few minutes, after vigorous effort, a strong arm had lifted her from her perilous position, and they saw each other for the first time, the youth and the maid. She told her story tremblingly, and every word she uttered only increased his interest and aroused his sympathy. He thought he had never seen one so good and fair, and took no pains to conceal his admiration.

"Say no more," she exclaimed; "you are strong and brave, and have rescued me from death. My heart goes strongly toward you. But this is no time and place for further talk. I am a poor Jewish girl of lowly parentage. If you would woo me, come to my house, and see my father and mother, as is the custom in Israel. And now, good youth, let me hasten to them. They are frantic, perhaps, at my long absence. Thanks, a thousand thanks for your brave deed ! "

"I am of a priestly family in Israel," he rejoined, proudly, "and would marry you, if you would give your consent. Let me first have a pledge from you, before I ask your parents."

"Do you wish a pledge of our betrothal?" she replied, half roguishly. "Why, here are witnesses. Let that weasel, which is running across the path and hears our talk, be a witness. Let the well, from which you rescued me, be a witness. And if you need a third witness, look at that bright star ahead of us. It shone on me so friendly when I was in peril. Let the star there be our third witness." And so they parted—he, to his duties and rich possessions; she, to her humble abode. Would they ever meet again?

A week had elapsed since her deliverance from the well. Each day she expected the youth, but he never came. She tried to excuse him—he was busy, no doubt, and lived at some distance, but his neglect was strange. A month glided by, and still no word from him. What did it mean? Was he faithless? Had he forgotten her? Impossible! He had risked his life to save hers, and the memory of his courage silenced the reproaches which were beginning to stir within her at his apparent indifference.

It was a painful struggle, as month followed month and year followed year. No complaint was heard. She kept her sorrow to herself, but she refused to mingle in the society of her little village. The attentions that her beauty

won grew distasteful. Many suitors appealed
for her hand, but they were dismissed in quick
succession. Her parents were surprised and
grieved, but that was of no avail. They could
not understand her mysterious behavior, and she
would not explain it, although she loved them
passionately. She must be ill—perhaps her
reason was giving way, due to her accident at
the well.

So the rumor spread that her mind was af-
fected; and only too glad that she was now in
no danger of being sought in marriage, she
strove to confirm the report by eccentricities
of manner and dress, which aroused the general compassion of the neighborhood. Would
the people have been as compassionate if they
had known the truth, and how in the silence of
her room she wept bitter tears as she thought
of her lover? But she did not lose her faith.
He would return to her and woo her as he had
promised. Were there not three witnesses of
their betrothal?

The maiden was happy in her ignorance—
for the youth was faithless. He had married
one of his own rank and station, and was sur-

rounded by every luxury, while a laughing babe gladdened him and his wife. One day, as it was asleep in its cradle, the mother for a moment left the room to perform some household duty. When she returned, what was her horror to find the infant dead, its little throat pierced by a weasel's fangs ! She never forgot the death of her first-born, and when the second babe came she watched it constantly, as if to guard it from some hidden foe. It was a strong, healthy boy, and grew rapidly under his mother's tender care. She never left him —day and night he was with her. He had reached his third year and his mother's fears were passing away, when, one afternoon, he ran out into the garden unobserved. Rushing to the well, which was unguarded, he fell in and was drowned, before his agonized parents were aware of his danger.

A few weeks had passed. It was early evening. The mother, whose fears had again been awakened by the sudden death of the child, felt positive that there was some mystery, which her husband alone could explain.

"Husband," she said, as they sat together

by the open door, "what curse is on thy life ?
Why have our two babes been snatched from
us by such dreadful deaths ? Tell me. Thou
knowest the reason. Conceal nothing from
me. There has been too much concealment
already, and my children have paid the penalty." And she wept aloud in her grief.

"Nay, wife," he replied, "do not weep. It
makes my agony the harder to bear."

"Husband," she repeated, "thou wilt nou
look me straight in the face. Thy eyes avoid
mine. Tell me the truth. Reveal the secret,
I adjure thee by our wedded troth !"

He could not resist her pleading gaze, but
told her all. She listened intently to the recital; not a word escaped her notice. Every
incident seemed photographed on her brain—
she saw the maiden in the well, heard her cries
for help, joined in her rescue, and caught the
words which plighted her to her deliverer.
The husband was reaching the end of the story.
His tones grew fainter as he spoke of the witnesses, the weasel, the well, and the star.

"Oh, husband !" she exclaimed, pressing her
hand to her heart, " see that bright star over-

head ! It is piercing me ! It has killed me !
Thy sin has been expiated at last. Seek the
one whom thou didst rescue and save her now
from despair and death. Go. Delay no longer."
And she sank back lifeless, as the bright star
seemed to vanish in the distant heavens.

When the man entered the village and inquired for the parents of the maiden, he was
met by such strange looks that he asked the
reason. They then told him of the girl's odd
behavior and how she refused to see anybody.
No one seemed to understand the cause of her
peculiar illness, which had lasted some time.
Her parents had sought the best medical advice, but without avail. She regarded every
stranger with suspicion, and resented all inquiries. She kept to herself, and her parents
were happy that she continued calm. She had
doubtless received some mental shock, and
they traced it to her accident in the well sev-
eral years previously.

Glad at least to learn that she was alive, and
rightly interpreting her behavior as indicating
her loyalty to him, who was unworthy of her

ardent faith, he sought an interview with her
parents and begged to be allowed to see their
daughter. At first they were not inclined to
consent, not wishing to torture her by permit-
ting a stranger to enter her presence. He was,
however, so persistent, and spoke so confidently of his ability to cure mental disease,
with which their daughter was afflicted, that
they reluctantly yielded.

She had not changed much. Her beauty
was still preserved. He recognized her at
once, but she failed to see in the cold, calm
stranger the impassioned youth who had delivered her from death. He assumed a critical
attitude, stood at some distance from her, then
came nearer, and uttering in a low voice, for
her alone, the words, " Three witnesses — star,
well, weasel !" left the room rapidly, followed
by her parents, who were completely mystified by his actions.

Who can attempt to describe her joy and
wonderment at the voice and words ? She restrained herself until she was left alone, and
then her thanksgiving was devout, while the
happy tears could not be held back. At last,

at last, after years of waiting, he had come to redeem his pledge. They were but moments, not years now. All doubts were removed, all misgivings set at rest. Her eyes beamed as brightly as in her early maidenhood, fresh color came into her cheeks, her listlessness and melancholy left her, and she was her own bright self once more.

Her parents, astounded and delighted at the change, ascribed everything to the strange physician and begged him to continue his visits until her health was fully restored. He gladly acceded to their request, and they were rejoiced to note how much stronger and happier their daughter grew, when once his identity was established and she learned that he loved her as of yore.

A week had passed and the man felt that he could deceive her parents no longer. Gathering courage from the strength of her affection and the nobility of her character, he told them that he had a secret to impart, and revealed his history. He did not spare himself and his faithlessness. When he spoke of his wife and his children, they could not restrain their tears. He related the story of their deaths, and wondered why they had suffered when he was to blame. Then he described his wife's last words, urging him to seek the maiden to whom he had plighted his troth and to rescue her again from despair which was worse than death.

"You have expiated your error, my son," the father said, deeply moved. "We cannot question the ways of God's providence. You, too, have suffered. And now you have come to make full atonement. Let my daughter, whom you once so cruelly deceived, decide whether the expiation is complete."

"I have already decided," she said, clasping his hand. "He was betrothed to me in righteousness and in justice, in loving-kindness and mercy. I never lost my faith in him. Let righteousness and mercy, let justice and loving-kindness be our witnesses forever!"

A STRING OF PEARLS.

IN a year when prices were high, a pious
man gave money to a wandering beggar.
His wife, a veritable Xanthippe, so upbraided
him for his act of kindness, that he fled from
home, and spent the night—it was New Year's
—in the graveyard. There, in the hush and
stillness of the hour, he heard the departed
souls of two maidens hold converse.

"Fly with me, dear sister," said the one,
"through airy space to heaven, that we may
learn the fate of the coming year."

"How can I leave the grave?" the other replied. "I have not been buried in garments
suited for so long a flight. Go thou alone,
and let me know what thou hearest."

Soon the maiden's soul returned, with the
information that in the coming year the early
harvest would be destroyed by hail, but the

late harvest would prosper. The pious man heard their talk, and as he was a prudent farmer, he acted accordingly, making wise provision for the future. In the meanwhile, he and his wife were on good terms again, but he could not resist the temptation to pass the next New Year's night in the same graveyard. Again, in the silence of the place, he heard the souls of the maidens in mysterious converse, but now their story was reversed. During the coming year the early harvest was to flourish, but the late harvest would be destroyed by a scorching wind. Again, the man knew how to profit by their colloquy; and, while all his neighbors complained of their bad fortune, his crops were richly blessed.

Now, the man's wife possessed all the curiosity of Bluebeard's spouse. She asked her husband the secret of his extraordinary good luck, and he told her, with much pride. Filled with the news—such a choice morsel was not hers every day—she hastened to the mother of the maiden buried in such unsightly fashion, and reviled her for her conduct; then returned home, thoroughly self-satisfied. Once more the New Year arrived, and again the pious man spent the night in the graveyard. But when a tremulous maiden-soul asked its companion to accompany it through space, the poor child rejoined, "Let me rest! Let me rest! The living have heard what we have here spoken in secret." The man strained every nerve; he caught no other sound but the sighing breeze.

A king had in his garden a yawning pit of great magnitude. One day he hired a number of workmen to fill it up. Some of them went to the sides of the pit, and as they saw its depth they exclaimed, "How is it possible to fill it?" and they gave up the work in despair. But the others said, "What matters it how deep it is? We are engaged by the day, and are happy to have something to do. Let us be faithful in our duty, and we will fill the pit as soon as we possibly can." Let no man say: "How immeasurable is the divine law! it is deeper than the sea; how many statutes to be performed! how can we carry them out and obey every command?" God says to man, "Thou art engaged by the day; do the work which thou canst, and think of naught else."

A prince once distributed costly garments among his slaves. The wise ones kept theirs carefully, but the foolish wore theirs even on work-days. Suddenly the prince summoned his slaves to a special audience, and said: "I wish to see again the clothes which I gave you." The garments of the wise slaves were clean, without a fold or stain; but the attire of the foolish slaves was stained and spoilt. Earnestly then rang out his words: "Ye wise ones, take your garments home and live in peace. Ye foolish ones, cast them into the fire to cleanse them!" Let thy soul—such is the meaning of the parable—return to its Maker as pure as when given thee. God may summon it at any moment. Be ever ready for the call.

As poetical is the rabbinical legend about David's harp. The royal Psalmist slept but little; he gave precious hours to the study of God's law. Over his bed he hung his harp, and at midnight, moved by the north wind, it poured forth of itself sweet melody. Aroused by the sound, David sprang from his couch, and spent the rest of the night in study and in song. Could the rabbis have told more impressively how the Psalms were the melody of David's soul, stirred by pious emotion?

To illustrate benevolence as a typical virtue of womankind, the story is told of Rabbi Hillel's wife, that once a poor man came to her and piteously begged for food. Seeing his famished state, she impulsively gave him all that she had on hand, and then quietly set to work to prepare a fresh meal. When dinner was ready, Hillel asked his wife the reason of the delay. She told him, unabashed, what she had done, and her husband blessed her for her true piety and kindliness.

The rabbis were not only teachers, but traders as well, carrying on various kinds of business for their livelihood. That they were not so very close at a bargain, a suggestive story would prove. A rabbi, while engaged in prayer, was approached by a customer who offered a certain price for some goods. He continued his devotions undisturbed. In his eagerness the man doubled his offer, thinking that the rabbi's silence was due to his being dissatisfied with the first price. In the meantime, the prayer came to an end, and the rabbi sold the goods at the first price offered. He was satisfied with it, and only on account of his prayers could give no answer.

When Herodotus told about the ring of Polycrates, he hardly imagined that the *Talmud* could furnish a parallel. The story is a practical argument in favor of Sabbath observance. There lived once a righteous Israelite, whose scrupulous regard for the Sabbath was widely known. It was a day he held in such high honor that he spared no cost to give it a holiday aspect. The Sabbath among the Jews was never a day of gloomy asceticism; manual labor and needless exertion were forbidden; but the atmosphere was a bright and joyous one. In the Israelite's vicinity lived a heathen of great wealth. It was foretold to the latter that his property should fall into the Jew's hands. Determined to thwart prophecy, he sold all his fortune for a precious gem, which he sewed in his turban, so that he might always have his property with him. Once, while crossing a bridge, the breeze blew his turban into the water, and with it he lost his dearly prized jewel. The next day a large fish was brought to market, and, as the Israelite wished to have it for his Sabbath meal, he secured it at a high price. On opening it, the jewel was found, which made him wealthy for all time.

The special sanctity attached to the Sabbath is farther illustrated in a story told of the Emperor Antoninus and Rabbi Judah the Holy. They were on friendly terms with each other, and one Sabbath the emperor dined with the rabbi and found the cold food very appetizing. He chanced to eat at the rabbi's house another time—it was on a week day—and although the hot repast was varied and costly, this did not taste as well as the other. " Wilt thou tell me, rabbi," the emperor asked, with a curiosity which was excusable in the monarch of Rome, "what made the cold food so appetizing ? " " There was a certain spice used in its preparation," the rabbi replied, " which is called Sabbath, and gives every dish a pleasant flavor." " Let me see it," the emperor answered quickly. "I would very much like to have it used in my kitchen." "This precious spice," said the rabbi, "is only to be used by those who keep the Sabbath day holy."

A fair specimen of rabbinical fancy is the following. The world contains ten hard things. The mountain is hard; iron pierces it. Iron is hard; fire melts it. Fire is hard; water extinguishes it. Water is hard; the cloud carries it. The cloud is hard; the air disperses it. The air is hard; man endures it. Man is hard; care bends him. Care is hard; wine banishes it. Wine is hard; sleep conquers it. But death is harder than all things; and still Solomon maintains, "Benevolence rescues from death."

The arrival of the king was anxiously awaited in a city. The streets were full of people, all eager to catch a glimpse of their ruler's face. A blind rabbi, Sheshet by name, mingled in the jostling crowd. Next to him stood a man who said scornfully, "Whole pitchers may go to the well — what do broken ones want?" The rabbi observed that the words were applied to him on account of his blindness, and answered softly, "Be calm, my friend; you will soon be convinced that I see better than you." Amid great noise a procession approached. "The king comes," the man exclaimed. "No," said the rabbi, "that is not the king." A second train of men drew near, amid the wildest uproar. "Now it is the king," said the man, confidently. "No," replied the rabbi, "again you are mistaken." At last a third procession approached and a solemn stillness prevailed. "Now the king has arrived," said the rabbi, and it was truly so. "How can you know this in your blindness?" asked the man, amazed. "An earthly sovereign," rejoined the rabbi, "resembles the heavenly Monarch. When God appeared in the wilderness to the prophet Elijah, there were storm, fire, and earthquake. Yet in all these violent manifestations of nature, the Deity approached not. It was only when a light breeze stirred that the prophet heard the voice of God."

A rabbi went out walking with some friends, and crossing a field he stopped and pointing to a beautiful vineyard, said, "This was mine, and I sold it for the poor, so that I might wholly devote myself to study." Going further, he pointed to a spacious field : " This too was mine," he exclaimed, " but I sold it, so as to have no other care than my holy studies." A few minutes' walk brought them to another field. " This was my last possession," he said, " but I gave it up so that I might have no other thought than the study of the Law." His friends, saddened at his words, which they regarded as showing an absolute want of prudence, replied : " What hast thou preserved for thy old age?" " Are you anxious on that account?" said he, smiling. " Why, I have resigned things which are given us only for a few days, for a possession that will last much longer."

Once a sage met the prophet Elijah in the crowded market-place, and full of curiosity he asked Elijah who of all the bustling throng would be saved. " None," replied the prophet, slowly. " What ! " the sage exclaimed, " no one of all these people?" At this moment two men entered the street and mingled with the crowd. They seemed in humble circumstances and no one noticed them or bade them greeting. "These will be saved," said the prophet in a low voice. The sage advancing toward them asked: "Will ye not kindly tell me what is your occupation in life? What are your virtues? What are your deeds?" "Virtues! deeds!" they replied, astounded. "In truth thou must be confounding us with somebody else. We are poor people and live by the work of our hands. Our only merit is is that we have merry hearts. When we meet one who is sad, we strive to chase away his sorrow. When we learn of two who are at enmity, we step in and try to make peace. This is our life-work." The men soon were lost in the crowd, but the sage did not forget their words.

When the Egyptians sank into the sea, the angels prepared to sing a hymn of joy. Then God spoke in His anger : "My creatures have sunk into the sea, and ye would sing a triumphant song!" When the hour for heathenism's fall draws nigh, so as to make room for Israel's triumph, Heaven will exclaim, "Both are my creatures: shall I destroy one for the other ?" The Lord assured Moses : "Israelite or heathen, man or woman, servant or freeman, all are equal in my sight; every good deed has its reward."

One day Hillel was seen by some of his disciples walking rapidly along the road. "Where are you going ?" they asked. "I am going to perform a commandment," he replied gently. "Tell us, master," they asked, "what special commandment ?" "Why," he rejoined, "it is to bathe myself in the bath-house." Full of curiosity, they inquired, "Is that one of the commandments ?" "Yes, indeed," Hillel answered. "If the statues of kings which are placed in the theatres and circuses must be kept clean and washed, how much more should I keep my body clean, for are we not all created in the image of God ?"

Rabbi Akiba once taught for a time in the morning under a large fig-tree. When the fruit grew ripe, the owner went out very early and gathered the ripe figs. The rabbi thought the honesty of himself and his disciples was suspected, and so chose another spot. The owner, troubled that they had gone, sought them out and asked why they had left his place. The rabbi told him the reason. " I did not suspect you," he quickly replied. " Return, I entreat you." They returned and the next morning the owner did not gather the figs; and when the sunbeams fell upon the tree, the ripe fruit became full of worms. "Now you see," said the owner, " why I plucked the fruit—because I did not desire it to be destroyed." " And now you see," said Rabbi Akiba to his disciples, "the full force of the words in the Song of Songs (vi. 2), ' My beloved is gone down to his garden to gather lilies.' Just as the owner of the fig-tree knows the exact time when his fruit must be gathered, so God knows when the righteous are to be taken from the world."

A certain rabbi once bought a camel of a wandering Arab, and his disciples took it in charge. Fancy their surprise, however, on removing the saddle, to discover a string of diamonds. " Master ! " they exclaimed in their excitement, "thou art favored by providence. Here is wealth as a reward for thy merits." " My pupils," rejoined the rabbi, " delay not a moment. Take back the diamonds to the man who sold me the animal. I bought a camel— not precious stones." The owner was not a little surprised to receive his diamonds, and blessed the rabbi for his honesty.

"Why do ye not rustle?" the fruit-trees were once asked. "Why should we make a noise?" they answered. "We do not need to attract attention. Our fruit testify in our favor." "Why do ye stir and rustle so much?" the forest trees were once questioned. "If we did not make a noise," they rejoined, "we would not be noticed at all."

Man has three friends—children and other relatives, wealth, and the good deeds he has performed. When he is near his death, he calls his first friend and beseeches his help. "I cannot help you," is the reply. "Does it not read in the Bible, 'Brother cannot redeem brother'?" He turns to the second friend, who says, "Scripture writes, 'Wealth is of no avail in the day of wrath.'" Finally he appeals to his good deeds, who answer, "When you approach God's judgment seat, you will find us there, and we will speak in your favor, as it is written, 'Thy righteousness will advance before thee when the glory of God receives thee.'"

"Here," said an Athenian to a Hebrew lad, "take this small coin, and purchase something for it, of which I may eat enough, leave a little for my host, and carry home a bit for my children." The lad quickly went and brought back salt. "Why didst thou purchase this?" the Athenian asked in anger. "I did not mention salt." "I am only obeying thy instructions," was the answer with a laugh. "Here is something of which thou mayst eat, leave some behind, and have a bit besides for thy little ones."

How remarkably — so reads a rabbinical thought—has the tongue been provided for in the economy of nature! Its position is carefully guarded, being placed within the mouth. To restrain it within its natural bounds, it has two outer walls — teeth and lips. To cool its intense ardor, it has been surrounded by a special streamlet—the salivary glands. Yet despite all these great precautions exercised, how readily does it occasion mischief. what fierce flame it arouses, what wretchedness does it cause !

A learned rabbi was walking one day amid the ruins of Jerusalem, accompanied by a friend. When he passed the spot where formerly the Temple stood in all its splendor, "Alas!" he cried, "the Temple, where we atoned for our sins, has fallen. How now shall we find atonement?" "Do not trouble thyself, master," said his friend gently. "A powerful means of atonement is left us. Benevolence will serve instead of offerings."

When it was decreed that the Law should be announced from the summit of a mountain, great was the rivalry among the mountains of the earth. Each desired the honor for itself, and was loud in its own praise. Then was heard a voice which said: "Ye are mountains, but ye are stained. Upon your heights altars have arisen, and smoke has ascended in worship of idols. Sinai alone is unstained, and from its crest shall resound the Divine word."

Rabbi Gamaliel, head of the academy, celebrated his son's wedding, and among his guests were three rabbis, Elieser, Joshua, and Sadok.

Gamaliel handed a goblet of wine to Elieser, who did not accept it, being unwilling to be served by so eminent a scholar. It was ne:... offered to Joshua, who quaffed it without a mo-ment's hesitation. " Is it proper," said Elieser to Joshua, " that we are seated comfortably here, and allow ourselves to be waited on by our master ? " " I know a greater man," Joshua rejoined, " who waited on his guests. Did not the patriarch Abraham wait upon vis-itors who he thought to be Arabian travelers, not angels ? " " How long," Sadok observed, " will you talk about the honor of mankind and forget the glory of the Creator ? Does not God wait upon humanity ? Does He not let the winds blow and the clouds descend ? Does He not send rain to fructify the soil, that plants may spring forth ? Does He not then set the table for every living being ? "

For *every* living being ! That was the uni-versalism of the rabbis, and while, in times of sharp distress and bitter recrimination, their utterances were human in their passion and agony, that spirit of broad humanity was never

wholly absent. " A heathen," said Rabbi
Meir, " who occupies himself with the law of
God stands in the same rank as the high priest."

THE VANISHED BRIDEGROOM.

IT was the moment of supremest pleasure to Abner. The wedding canopy had been raised, the benediction uttered, the ring placed on the bride's finger, the kiss given to seal the union. She was his own at last; his highest ambition had been gratified. With words of congratulation his friends crowded around him; it was a joyous atmosphere, indeed, while his wife gazed at him with the love-light in her eyes.

"Dearest," he exclaimed, suddenly, as he withdrew with her for a moment to a corner of the apartment which overlooked the garden with its winding paths, from which strains of music arose, inviting all to the dance; "dearest, I must leave thee now."

"O Abner," the bride half sobbed in reply, "wouldst thou leave me at this moment of all moments in the world? Why, the echoes of the marriage blessings still resound in the air.

Whither wouldst thou go, dearest? Surely," she added, with a look of reproach, "thy place is now at my side. Wouldst thou forsake me on our wedding day?"

"Nay, my beloved; make no close inquiry, nor seek to restrain me. I must go. I have sworn to go. Only trust in me, and doubt not my faithfulness. I shall return within an hour, and then explain all to thee. Have no fear for my sake." And without further farewell than a quick embrace, Abner left her and hurried into the open air before the astonished guests could realize that the bridegroom was missing.

* * *

Of all the youth in Jerusalem, Abner and Caleb were the comeliest lads, and their friendship had grown into a proverb. Close companions at school from boyhood to early manhood, no love could have been more tender, no sympathy more profound, than that which made them kindred spirits. They were fond of the same pleasures, they shared the same dreams, their studies and occupations were alike, their aspirations identical. They loved to give free rein to their fancies with youth's rapt enthusiasm, and build such dream palaces that the magic splendor of Solomon's creations paled in comparison. What a daring architect is youth! It knows not the impossible. It bridges the chasm of infinite time; it rears a structure to the highest heaven. It summons to its aid principalities and powers, and never acknowledges defeat. Love and hope and faith are the patient genii who at its exultant bidding transform earth and sky.

Among the topics which Abner and Caleb were fond of discussing as they grew to maturity, the future life and immortality most strongly appealed to them. The fact that it was but dimly foreshadowed in the Law and the Prophets added to its fascination, and the rare references to it in the debates of the schools only increased its hold upon them. One day, in the heat of their arguments, Caleb, more impassioned than usual, seized his companion's hand.

"Abner," he exclaimed, "wouldst thou know the secrets of eternal life?"

"Why, Caleb," Abner rejoined, moved by his friend's earnestness, "what a strange question to ask! How can we mortals understand aught of immortality? Does not our Law say that 'the secret things belong to the Lord'?"

"Faith can pierce all barriers, dear friend," Caleb answered, impressively, "and love, though buried from sight, can make its own revelation."

"What dost thou mean, Caleb, by those mysterious words and thrilling tones?" Abner inquired, deeply stirred, for he felt that never before had their conversation been so earnest.

"Dost thou not believe, Abner, in immortality?"

"Surely, Caleb, I do, as the central conviction of my nature."

"If this is thy belief, then, may not the immortal spirit seek converse with mortality and minister to the wants and desires of mortal flesh on earth?"

"Caleb, thou shouldst not speak in this strain. It is almost blasphemy. Think of the fate of the sons of Aaron, who brought strange fire into the sanctuary."

"Nay, Abner, I am guilty of no blasphemy. I am convinced that those who pass from life do not become as petrified as the slabs that cover them. They hover around those who loved them and whom they loved on earth, and mingle in their joys and sorrows."

"It must be so, Caleb, if thou thinkest so," said Abner, after a pause.

"Come, Abner," Caleb solemnly exclaimed, "let us swear by the Eternal that if either of us die the survivor shall seek to communicate with the departed one and visit the sepulchre at the moment of his highest happiness on earth. Then it is my fervent belief that the secret of heavenly happiness will be unfolded, and we shall attain the highest degree of intelligence."

The compact was made—an unusual thing in those days among the pious Jewish youth to invoke the Lord's name—and the conversation ended. In a few years Caleb died, and Abner, disconsolate and dejected, disdained for a while all society, but spent the largest share of his leisure at the friend's grave, reflecting on his genial traits and their loving intercourse. Time, however, works its magical changes, and now he had married.

*　*　*

"I had almost forgotten thee, beloved Caleb," said Abner softly to himself, as he left the crowded streets of Jerusalem, and gained the roadway leading to the cemetery. "Surely this is the happiest moment of my life, wedded to the one I hold most dear. Could there be a more fitting time to think of thee and our mutual oath?"

It did not take long, for the distance was short and he walked with hurried steps, before Abner found himself close to the simple slab that covered the remains of Caleb. Flinging himself upon it, he gave way to his emotions, but by a strong effort his self-control gained the mastery. Then he communed thus with the spirit of his friend:

"Beloved Caleb, not with fear and trembling, but with glad confidence I approach thee. Thou rememberest our oath. I have come to thy grave at the full tide of my happiness, to learn of thy experience in the realms of bliss. Thou recallest our converse in those joyous days of youth when it was our desire to pierce all mystery. Be near to me now, dear friend, and in thy purified state uplift the veil which hides the mortal from the immortal. Inspire me now, O Caleb, with the knowledge I seek, and let me not ask in vain."

Abner ceased, half expectant of some response. But no voice broke the stillness. The shadows of evening were deepening. One by one the stars shone in the firmament. Abner failed to notice the advancing night in his rapt contemplation. Then a faint murmuring rent the air, and the trees that skirted the burial ground seemed to give forth a sobbing sound.

"O Caleb," Abner entreated, with oustretched hands, "answer me. By the ineffable name of God, answer me."

The tremulous weeping of a child was borne on the breeze. A flash of lightning lit up the distant hills, and a rumbling as of thunder was heard.

"Do I disturb thee, O Caleb, from thy rest? Forgive me, beloved friend. But answer me, as thou didst swear to do. Tell me the delights of immortal life."

"Abner, Abner!" At the words Abner's countenance shone with sudden joy. "At last!" he exclaimed, "at last, I hear thy voice again."

"Abner, such a delight is mine as is comparable truly to no earthly bliss. So pure, so radiant, so serene, are my companions that my voice cannot describe a thousandth portion of my happiness. Have no regret at our severed friendship. A sweeter, stronger bond unites us now. Dost thou yearn to see again my features and clasp my hands as of old? Why, I am nearer to thee than in the past, and my eye sees clearer within where spirit responds to spirit and all is at perfect peace. I have solved the mystery. I have gained the heights."

The voice ceased for a moment, and then it resumed:

"More could I tell thee. But dost thou know the penalty? A thousand years on earth are but as a moment in eternity. Even as thou communest with me here, beloved friend, the years vanish and life recedes. Ah, hasten, hasten, ere it be too late. Thy bride awaits thee and wonders why thou art tarrying. Wouldst thou learn the secret of eternal life? Make thy earth a heaven and live well thy mortal years, with their alternate sunshine and shade, as best preparation for immortality! Heaven begins on earth —there is no chasm between the two worlds. But hasten, hasten! I dare speak no more, for thine own dear sake."

Again a child's tremulous wail was borne to Abner's ear. There came a flash of lightning and the muttering of thunder. Then the shadows lifted, and it was sunrise on earth, with a fresh, cheerful air sweeping across the hills.

"Why, I have been sleeping," Abner exclaimed, rising with difficulty from the ground. "How careless on my part! My limbs are as stiff as an old man's, and my shaggy beard has grown over night! A pretty figure to meet my bride," he muttered, as he moved with hesitating steps toward Jerusalem. He gained the old roadway, although its lines had changed. He did not recognize the fields in which some peasants were ploughing, while on every side were scattered débris and heaps of stone.

"Almighty!" he entreated, as he strained his sight for the accustomed glory of the temple mount. "Where art thou vanished, O Jerusalem? O beloved bride, shall I see thee no more? Must I pay such a penalty for a moment's bliss? Home, friends, country—have I lost ye all?"

Abner had dreamed seventy years, and when the dream-cloud had lifted, bride and friends had long since died. The Temple had fallen and

Jerusalem had become a ruin—the spoil of triumphant Rome.

In seeking to pierce the mysteries of the future, the present had passed from view, and left Abner in solitude—that was the penalty of seeing visions.

THE LESSON OF THE HARVEST.

IT was late afternoon in harvest time, and the fields were full of golden glory. In the genial climate of Samaria each year the wheat and corn ripened as luxuriantly as flower and fruit. But of all the farmers, the choicest harvest seemed to come to Abdon's field of corn, from year to year. How the man's heart swelled with gratitude as he strolled up and down with his son in the invigorating air! It would be soon sunset. It was already cooler, and delicious rest would be their good fortune that night.

"Joash, the priest, was here this morning, my son," Abdon said, gazing fondly at the outspread field, "and I told him that I would have the tithe sent in a day or two. This year I shall have at least a thousand sheaves—it has been a bountiful season—and I shall set aside one-tenth for holy use."

"But, father," the son exclaimed a little impatiently, "would not fifty suffice? Why give away so much?"

"Nay, Caleb, my son. That is not spoken with your usual wisdom. The tenth part of our produce shall be the Lord's, so runs the olden mandate. Is that too much to return to the Lord for all His bounty? Does He not give us the rich harvest, does He not send sunshine and rain, wind and calm, summer and winter? Where would we be without His watchful care day and night? One hundred sheaves will be taken for the sanctuary as our grateful offering and happy, thrice happy am I, that we can give so much!"

"But, father," the son again protested, "surely we might save half of that and put it aside for the future. Corn is growing more valuable, and the money will enable us to enlarge our home, will it not?"

"The Lord has not abandoned us, nor has His power weakened, that we should distrust His providence. My son, would it not be robbery to withhold from one what is his due?"

"Certainly, father. That admits of no doubt."

"Then, Caleb, it is robbery to withhold from the Almighty the tenth that is His. And suppose we were to enlarge our house by such ill-gotten gains. Why, it would be a den of thieves, accursed, unholy." And Abdon's voice trembled in his agitation.

"Forgive me, father, if I have disquieted you," Caleb replied, with heightened color. "I know that the earth and all its produce are the Lord's, but I did not think it necessary to bestow so much on the tabernacle."

"My dearest son," Abdon answered slowly, "make this your rule in life—never begrudge what you give to the tabernacle, the gifts of a loving, grateful heart in the service of God and man. Come, let us return."

The months passed swiftly, and one day Abdon, who was beginning to feel the increasing weaknesses of age—he was over seventy—realized that his end was approaching. So he called one evening his son to his bedside, and kissing him warmly, said, "My beloved son, the time is at hand when my spirit will return to Him who gave it. I feel the weight of my years. I cannot remain much longer on earth. You must know this, without any word of mine."

"Father, father," sobbed the son. "Father, do not tell me this. You are strong for your years.

You have rarely had a day of illness. God will not take you from us."

"My son," Abdon continued in a firm, clear tone, "obey God's voice in all things. Follow the righteous path laid down by our sages. Forget not, whatever happens, to give to the sanctuary one-tenth each year of all your wealth, as God has commanded us. And so the Almighty's blessing will rest on you, and you and yours will be happy in the love of God and man."

He kissed his son and bade him good night. And in the morning, the father, so loving and righteous, passed away.

The son's grief was sincere. He mourned according to the customs of his people. He missed the father deeply, and the dwelling seemed a solitude now that he was seen no more. His kindly voice, his pious ways, his earnest counsel, his daily benediction—these had become a memory.

"I shall obey my father's instructions," said Caleb to himself. "I shall give the full tenth of my produce to the priests for the tabernacle. May the Almighty bestow upon me a share of my father's gracious spirit!"

The first year the field bore a magnificent crop of corn—it was the wonder and admiration of his neighbors. The corn stood high and waved with each passing breeze as if in devout thankfulness to the Maker of seed time and harvest, summer and winter. It yielded a thousand sheaves, and Caleb sent promptly the tenth part to the priest, who thanked him for his piety. And his friends among themselves were never weary of repeating his praise.

Who can foresee the workings of the human heart? Who can foretell the contrary winds that sweep out of its course the ship which leaves port so hopefully? And the day that opens so brightly, can we be certain that its radiance and charm long before evening will not vanish in storm and rain? Our best resolves, our ardent wishes for goodness—are these always permanent? Do they not often suffer a sad and sudden change?

The second year after his father's death, as Caleb was watching his field a month or more before the harvest, and was anticipating a still larger yield of corn to reward his labor, he said to himself, "What folly to give away what is

my own! It is my field, my corn, my toil each
day. What right have I to rob myself in mistaken piety? This year I shall be wiser. I shall
keep for myself every ear of corn. It is my
property."

The harvest came—it was a joyous scene
in every field. The labor of the season was
sweetened by song and dance, and the sanctuary was not forgotten by the grateful people.
But Caleb sent no offering. He kept all the
golden sheaves for himself. How his neighbors
wondered, and many seemed grieved. But they
kept their thoughts to themselves. Silence is
wisdom, reads the olden proverb.

The third year was in rapid flight. When we
are young, how slowly the years pace along! Each
minute is like an hour, and each month seems
without possibility of end. When we grow older,
each hour is like a minute, each month a week,
each year a day, so swiftly vanishes God's most
precious and least valued gift—time!

The harvest was now rapidly approaching. One
day, as Caleb was observing closely his field, he
noticed to his great surprise that the corn appeared hardly as sturdy as of old. It was cer-

tainly less luxuriant; there were empty patches here and there. In alarm he strove to thin out the less satisfactory portions, and by repeated waterings to give fresh life and vigor to the rest. Despite his efforts, early and late, in which he was aided by a large number of helpers, the harvest yield was only five hundred sheaves—half the produce of the previous year!

Great was his dismay as he saw how fruitless had been his toil. He had rarely experienced so bitter a disappointment. He resolved, however, that the following year would make ample amends and restore the old-time productiveness. He spared no pains. He hired efficient help. He applied every known method of improving the soil. There was not a day which found him absent from his post, watching every growth, destroying every apparent imperfection. And now when the harvest time neared, he felt confident that all would be well.

How keen was again his disappointment! The field, so carefully tilled and planted, yielded only one hundred sheaves. How could he now avert impending ruin and disgrace? How could he wrestle with such persistent misfortune? He had done his best—he must accept calmly the wreck of his fortune. Poverty was to be his life-companion—he upon whom prosperity had always smiled. In his despair he kept within his dwelling, half ashamed to meet his neighbors, and knowing with absolute certainty that the day was near when he would be obliged to sell home and field, and wander elsewhere for a livelihood. Such incidents were part of human life—but that he should be singled out for such a fate was crushing to a man of his pride and self-confidence.

It was a bright afternoon a few weeks after the harvest, and he was seated in his home, not in the best of humor, for he could not help thinking of the ruin that was impending, when a number of his friends appeared in the doorway. He ran to meet them, begging them to enter, but amazed to observe that they were in festal garments.

"Friends," was his startled exclamation, "what do you want? Why do you wear festal raiment? Have you come, perhaps, to feast your eyes on my poverty?" And he covered his face, as if in shame.

"Nay, Caleb," one of them replied, feelingly.

"You are mistaken. We have not come to mock you or to hold you to scorn. But we are wearing the same garments as when we took our tithes to the sanctuary. Would you learn why? It is to greet you as priest!"

"I a priest!" rejoined Caleb in amazement. "I a priest! You must be jesting, friends."

"No, we are not jesting, Caleb," came the answer. "We are here to aid you all we can. Our truest friends are those who point out to us firmly, yet kindly, our faults and weaknesses. And you, you alone, are to blame for all that has happened to you. It is your greed, your selfish nature, that has held you by an iron chain, and held you fast."

"Explain yourself," Caleb interrupted, indignantly. "What do you mean by such a charge?"

"It is true, every word. Did not your father bequeath to you a holy trust? Did he not on his deathbed entreat you to remember the source of your wealth, the bountiful Giver of Sunlight, wind, rain, and fertile soil? Did he not?" He paused for a moment, and then, without waiting for a reply, continued: "Your loving father, whose memory is an everlasting blessing, asked you almost with his last breath to give to the priest, as the law commands, one-tenth of your produce. So long as you obeyed, you prospered, did you not? God was the priest to whom you gave your tithe as owner of the corn. A hundred sheaves He received from you, and gave you nine hundred. Ah, if you had kept to that practice, the result would have been different. But the time came when your pride and greed led you astray, and you refused to pay your debt— the tenth part of your harvest. At once the Almighty, the creator and possessor of the whole earth, became the owner of the field, and you, Caleb, was but the priest with only a hundred sheaves as your share. Do you realize the change? Is the meaning clear?"

For a moment there was silence, and then Caleb, standing proudly erect, and extending to them his right hand, exclaimed:

"Friends and neighbors, I thank you sincerely for your rebuke. You are true friends. I shall try to profit by your words of reproof and wisdom. As for the Almighty, His ways are just. My eyes, so long blinded by my selfish greed, have been opened at last. Here in the presence of the Almighty God, and with you as witnesses, I solemnly vow to cherish my beloved father's counsel. Greed and pride shall no longer control my motives, but the fear of the Lord and the love of His law. And each year, whether the harvest be large or small, the tenth will be given to the sanctuary, the grateful offering of my humbled heart."

Joyfully his friends left the dwelling. Their mission was accomplished. They felt confident that Caleb would no more neglect his duties, and that prosperity would return to his home and field.

www.ingramcontent.com/pod-product-compliance
Lightning Source LLC
Chambersburg PA
CBHW020444270626
47155CB00022B/1416